WOMEN *of* DESTINY

LISA M. TAIT

WOMEN
of
DESTINY

FIVE PRINCIPLES FOR
PURSUING
YOUR PURPOSE IN GOD

LISA M. TAIT

FOREWORD *by*
TERESA HAIRSTON
PUBLISHER
GOSPEL TODAY MAGAZINE

Destiny House books are available for special promotions and premiums. For details contact Destiny House Special Markets, 5238 Ashley Dr., SW, Lilburn, GA 30046. Dr. Lisa Tait is available for speaking engagements by contacting her at www.womenofdestiny.org or call 770-356-0101.

WOMEN *of* DESTINY
FIVE PRINCIPLES FOR PURSUING YOUR PURPOSE IN GOD

Copyright © 2006 Lisa M. Tait
Published by Destiny House Publishers
P.O. Box 2227
Stone Mountain, Georgia 30086
www.womenofdestiny.org
ISBN-10: 1-59971-957-6
ISBN-13: 978-1-59971-957-6

Cover art and interior layout by Cristina Mershon

Interior Artwork by Andre Thompson

Wardrobe furnished by Horizon's Boutique, Fayetteville, GA

Cover Photography by Bill Ransom

Printed in the United States of America

THIS BOOK

DEDICATED TO

The *"Woman of Destiny"* who gave life to me, Gloria Wilson,

the *"Woman of Destiny"* God has given me to train up, Essence Ayana Tait,

to the loving men in my life who support me, Dr. Jerusa Wilson Sr., Dr. Lewis Tait, Jr., and Asante Tait, my loving brothers, Carl and Eric,

to my God-Partner friends, Dr. Sharon Curtis, Dr. Steve Bland, Jr., Dr. Teresa Hairston, Rev. Jocelyn Thornton, Dr. John W. Kinney,

to the Women of Destiny at the Imani Christian Center and to all women who are seeking to find meaning, and power to live their lives with majesty and beauty.

Women of Destiny
WALKING IN PURPOSE, PROMISE & POWER!

CONTENTS

FOREWORD

Mark Twain wrote, *"Plan for the future because that's where you are going to spend the rest of your life."* In today's society, every woman is challenged to embrace that precious commodity known as purpose. It is purpose that is the driving force behind success. In direct contrast, being unsure of one's purpose can be the cause of dismal failure at worst; or desperate seeking at best. In this book, Dr. Lisa Tait helps readers find the keys that will unlock the door to fulfillment, purpose and ultimately destiny.

Picking up this book is like grabbing hold of a rope while swimming in the midst of deep water. The five powerful principles presented here will give you the necessary power to take the next vital steps on your journey to your destiny.

Additionally, you should take advantage of the study questions at the end of each chapter. Use them as mental and spiritual motivators. And, if possible, create group settings where you can reflect on them.

Most of all, take note of the generous practical advice Dr. Lisa shares throughout this book. It is absolutely fascinating! Her life experiences will bless you.

As you journey toward that special "place" God has prepared for you, you will surely collect valuable treasures along the way. No matter how far down the road you get, there are times when you need to dig into your treasure chest and pull out a gem to refresh you. This book is one of the gems!

TERESA HAIRSTON
PUBLISHER, GOSPEL TODAY MAGAZINE

INTRODUCTION

I ndeed creation was not complete until God fashioned and breathed into woman the breath of life. It was then that God gave God's grand benediction over all creation and declared in Genesis 1:31 that it was *very good.* In fact, woman completed the circle of life and God's plan for humanity. Therefore given this reality why aren't we clear about our purpose, promise and power? Why are we finding ourselves in destructive and toxic relationships? Why are we so depressed and despondent and unable to achieve our goals? Why are we living beneath our promise and possibility? *Women of Destiny* was written to help women focus on the process of developing, shaping, and birthing purpose in their lives.

It is out of my own spiritual journey to discover and know myself that I have chosen to address the issue of women achieving spiritual self-actualization. Spiritual self-actualization is defined as achieving one's ultimate destiny in life; and recognizing one's power, authority and influence in the world.

I quickly discerned that if I, a woman who was afforded every opportunity to succeed in life (great parents, good education, economic stability, supportive siblings, and meaningful friendships), was struggling with becoming spiritually self-actualized that there must be others who wrestled with the same issue. I realized through my own personal journey that being lost, not knowing your purpose in life, and not using your gifts and talents fully for the kingdom was a horrible abyss. It was a dark, cold place filled with tears and pain. As I talked to other women in the church and outside of the church I quickly discerned that I wasn't the only one struggling to know self. I wasn't the only one unhappy with being unproductive. I wasn't the only woman who had given the authority for her destiny and the reins of her life over to someone else. I wasn't the only woman who ended each day feeling exhausted and unappreciated. In the five churches that I had found myself working in over the years, whether they were small or large, one reality resonated, and it was that women were searching. Although many of these women were successful in their careers, in their homes, in the community, in politics, and even in the church, many of them still could not answer the question, "Why did God create me? What is my life's purpose?" As I began to minister in a context with more women, I began to receive feedback that through my living, my preaching, my teaching, and my counseling, I was helping women discover their true being in God. And so I was faced with the sudden and swift reality that I would either have to ignore this charge to help women or I was going to have to develop a process or program to move women toward their destiny in God. Vision and purpose in our lives is often times birthed through our burdens. You might see someone living in the streets and suddenly a burden is placed upon your heart to reach out to the homeless. You may encounter a woman who is in an abusive relationship and the burden to free her is so great you dedicate your life to rescuing abused women and children. Well, this is the case with *Women of Destiny*. I felt a burden. I saw a need. I sensed a serious problem existing in the Christian community among women. This work is my attempt to lift that heavy burden.

THE BOOK'S PURPOSE

Given the reality that many women are not understanding and embracing their call in life due to historical, societal, and even religious constraints, and based on the Biblical premise that all should come into an understanding and acceptance of God's will for their lives, this book purposes to educate and empower women, thus enabling them to respond and ultimately fulfill God's call on their lives. The purpose of this book is to allow individuals and churches to minister to women who seek to discover their true identities and make the most of their God-given talents and gifts.

It is designed to be conducted as a Self-Study or Group-Study to be held over an eight-week period. The first chapter is primarily an introduction to the journey, the next six chapters encompass the five components of spiritual self-actualization and the final chapter brings closure and celebrates the call each woman has embraced for her life.

HOW TO READ THIS BOOK

Women of Destiny utilizes a systematic approach to awakening women to their raison d'être or reason for being. It is not simply a Bible study but instead a spiritual journey which requires great discipline and commitment. Each chapter is written to allow the reader to reflect on its contents, answer the "Growth through Contemplation" questions and journal one's thoughts, fears and concerns.

This book outlines what I believe to be God's Divine Paradigm for women discovering their person, partners, purpose, promise and power in God. This paradigm consists of five components. Each chapter corresponds to one of the five components of spiritual self-actualization outlined below. The five components of this paradigm are inter-connected and integral in their contribution toward spiritual self-actualization. It is my belief that we continually grow and develop in these five areas as we discover more about God and ourselves in order to attain spiritual self-actualization.

These components are:

1. God Produced - Women are able to define themselves and see that they are made in the image and likeness of God.

2. God Placed - Women come to discover their place in the world; "unmasking, disentangling and debunking systems of oppression that place restrictions and boundaries on them" (as stated by Dr. Katie Geneva Cannon).

3. God Partnered - Women recognize the importance of partnerships (i.e., sista-girlfriends, mentoring relationships, models for parenting, intimate relationships) with others that will ultimately enhance their ability to live out their purpose.

4. God Purposed - Women come to discover their reason for being (raison d'être) and fulfill their pre-determined function for humanity.

5. God Empowered - Women reach a place in their lives when they are embodied with power and authority from God; having spiritual power such that they are able to reach their God potential and spiritually self-actualize.

Each chapter begins with the story of a young woman who comes face to face with the reality of her existence. Cynthia struggles through the challenges of life in order to know self and finds herself struggling with loneliness, depression and addictions. In Chapter Two we find Karen who contends with discovering where her place is in a world that seems to classify and stratify African American, economically disadvantaged, women at the bottom of the totem pole. Chapter Three opens with the story of Toni and Lynn who were best friends until one of them began to achieve her goals and dreams. There friendship quickly began to disintegrate because neither of them truly understood dedication, friendship and loyalty. In Chapter Four we peer into the life of Patricia, a self-made woman who seemed to embody success yet deep down she was miserable, lonely and empty. Her life seemed to be an endless parade of meetings, power lunches, and networking, until she realized something had to change to give her life meaning. Finally in Chapter Five Tiffany, a young woman who struggled in the world of an abusive relationship finally emerges to find strength from her struggle and serve as a role model for other abused women. All of these women faced difficult challenges and hurdles which seemed at times to consume their very beings, however, through the power of God they transitioned from being victims to victors.

Their stories and the scripture lessons that follow are combined with the penetrating movie *"The Color Purple"* to teach life lessons on how we as women can come to know our purpose, promise and power in this world.

MY VOW & COMMITMENT

Through the power of God and the focus of my will and spirit, I vow to journey into the realm of self-discovery, self-love and purpose. I make this commitment as a woman with a divine destiny and purpose.

_____

YOUR NAME

_____

YOUR CHURCH/ORGANIZATION'S NAME

_____

LISA M. TAIT, D. MIN.

All our dreams can come true - if we have the courage to pursue them.

> *"Be strong and courageous and act,*
> *Do not fear nor be dismayed,*
> *For the Lord God, my God*
> *is with you.*
> 1 CHRONICLES 28:20

THE FIVE COMPONENTS

OF SPIRITUAL SELF-ACTUALIZATION

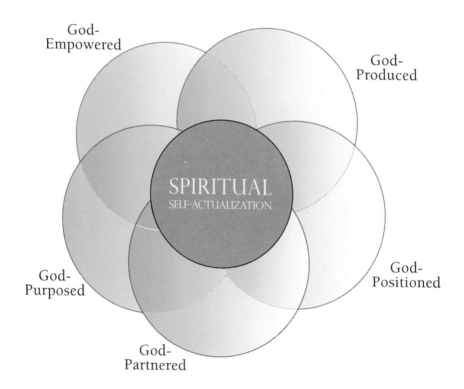

NOTE: Note: This diagram is created in such a way that the five components of being God-Produced, God-Positioned, God-Partnered, God-Purposed and God-Empowered are integral. These components are inter-connected in the spiritual lives of women such that we are always struggling to achieve balance in these areas in order to reach spiritual self-actualization. I believe that women naturally navigate through and achieve wholeness in these areas as long as they do not encounter insurmountable social or environmental hurdles. I believe that women are consciously motivated toward spiritual self-actualization and therefore they will struggle, tolerate pain, and search for clarity in order to ultimately reach this goal.

PROLOGUE

Women *of Destiny* is designed for women who are ready to move from mediocre to magnificent, from ordinary to extraordinary, from infertile with frustration to pregnant with possibility. This book was written for women who deeply desire to become a "Woman of Destiny." In order for this to be your heart's desire you must first however, be able to articulate what it means to be a "Woman of Destiny." We recognize that it sounds relevant, it sounds important, it even has a certain element of mystery to it, but what on earth does it mean to be a "Woman of Destiny?"

When we speak of *destiny* we are referring to a predetermined course of events or actions held or ordered by an irresistible power or agency. Therefore a "Woman of Destiny" is a woman whose life is predetermined and ordered by an irresistible power we call God. That's right women of destiny don't panic, they rarely complain, they keep a level head, they walk with a quite assurance, they speak with a voice of authority, they fear little, and they love greatly. This is all made possible because these women know deep down that their steps are ordered, their destiny is determined, their battles are already won, and their God is in charge. God created them in such a way, that no one or no-thing can derail, disrupt or destroy God's plan for their lives.

The good news is that *you* are that "Woman of Destiny." No matter who is plotting your destruction, or what illness is trying to claim you, or how much or little money you have in the bank, or how bad that relationship is, or how much those children are getting on your nerves, or if you're in between jobs, you have this assurance - no one or nothing can disrupt God's design for your life.

The Women of Destiny who have come before us, are women who have accomplished great feats, they are well-known trailblazers, successful educators, prolific preachers, bodacious businesswomen, profound public speakers, powerful politicians, our Mamas and Big Mamas. They are women like Harriet Tubman, Sojourner Truth, Mary McCloud Bethune, Jerena Lee, Bishop Vashti McKenzie, Shirley Chisholm, Maxine Waters, Fannie Lou Hamer, Toni Morrison, Bessie Smith, Mahalia Jackson, and Oprah Winfrey.

These women, like you, are in the elite company of what I call "Women of Destiny." These are women who never allowed their *situation* to dictate their *destination*. They fell down but they got back up, they made mistakes but they never stopped moving, they were talked about but they never listened to their enemies, and they got sick but they never stopped serving. These are the women Maya Angelou writes about in her poem "And Still I Rise."

> *You may write me down in history*
> With your bitter twisted lies,
> You may trod me in the very dirt
> But still, like dust I rise.

Does my sassiness upset you?
Why are you beset with gloom?
'Cause I walk like I've got oil wells
Pumping in my living room.

Just like moons and like suns,
With the certainty of tides,
Just like hopes springing high
Still I rise

Did you want to see me broken?
Bowed head and lowered eyes?
Shoulders falling down like teardrops,
Weakened by my soulful cries.

Does my haughtiness offend you?
Don't you take it awful hard
'Cause I laugh like I've got gold mines
Diggin in my own backyard.

You may shoot me with your words,
You may cut me with your eyes,
You may kill me with your hatefulness,
But still, like air, I'll rise.

Out of the huts of history shame
I rise
Up from a past that's rooted in pain
I rise

I'm a black ocean, leaping and wide
Welling and swelling I bear in the tide.
Leaving behind nights of terror and fear
I rise

Into a daybreak that's wondrously clear
I rise
Bringing the gifts that my ancestors gave,
I am the dream and hope of the slave.

I rise, I rise, I rise.

This book is not interested in addressing the concerns of any kind of woman; we want to deal specifically with "Women of Destiny." These are the kind of women who have left and will leave a legacy. Their lives have been threatened, doors have been closed in their face, they've felt the sting of discrimination because of their race, class and sex, and some have been sexually abused, while others have been abandoned. But these women never gave up, they kept on believing that God had ordered their steps and that no weapon formed against them would prosper, that greater was He that was in them than he who was in the world, that nothing could separate them from the love of God in Christ Jesus, and that failure was not an option because God could do anything but fail.

We are currently in a society that devalues women while celebrating a Hip-Hop culture that unashamedly refers to women as female dogs or prostitutes! And what is even sadder is that we have young women and children responding to these labels with a certain kind of pride. It is time for "Women of Destiny" to take a stand and show the world that we are not simply hips, lips, eyes and thighs! We are "Women of Destiny" who have been called for such a time as this. We have been called out and called up to a higher and grander purpose.

If you are willing to embark on this journey, embrace the concepts outlined in this book and apply them to your life you will soon discover your destiny. Your purpose is not a mystery, it is a well conceived and ordered plan for your life. However, you must be willing to do the work that is required to meet God face to face.

In my neighborhood we have a brand new Aquatics Center. In that large outdoor pool along with two huge water slides and a water playground, there is a river. The river is propelled by water such that all one has to do is get in the flow of the river and it will carry you around. This book is much like that river. If you can just get in the flow of what God wants to do in your life you will be propelled into peace, prosperity, power and potential. If you are ready let's begin this spiritual journey by looking at the scriptural tools that we have been given to become "Women of Destiny."

CHAPTER ONE

God–
PRODUCED

"So God created man in his own image, in the image of God created he him, male and female, created he them."
GENESIS 1: 27 (KJV)

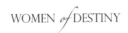

There she stood with all the trappings of success and power yet feeling as empty, void, and cold as any corpse in a hospital morgue. As she completed the finishing touches to her makeup, she realized for the first time that she had never really looked inside herself. Cynthia was well aware of the exterior picture, her make-up immaculate, her designer suit freshly laundered and pressed, her hair perfectly coifed. She was by all earthly standards a beautiful woman. But while she spent a lifetime looking in the mirror, she never looked beyond the mirror at the woman who stood ready to know and embrace self. As she departed her half-million dollar home, she climbed into her luxury automobile preparing for another long commute to the city from the suburbs. She dreaded the journey not only because of its length, the traffic, and its final destination but mainly because it left her with forty-five uninterrupted minutes to think about her life. Not even the intense volume of the radio could drown out the feelings of emptiness and confusion she felt. In the eyes of those around her Cynthia embodied complete and total success. She had already attained three degrees by the age of thirty-two, was working an upper-level management job, and had a wonderful salary to top it off. But little did those around her know how empty, depressed, and emotionally drained she was. Cynthia was ashamed to admit it but there were even times when she contemplated what the world would be like absent of her presence. She wasn't suicidal, but the emptiness of not knowing who she was caused her to feel nameless and faceless in a world full of personalities and reputations. As a tear raced down her face, finding itself hanging by her chin for dear life, she decided, "Not another day... I won't live like this another moment... I must discover who I truly am." In the depths of her pain, she found the courage to begin the process of change.

Cynthia's story is that of millions of women in our society. We possess all the trappings of success and fulfillment however; we are languishing in pits of low self-esteem, lack of self-knowledge and little self-respect. The Bible says, *"As a man (woman) thinketh, so is he (she)."* But what happens when you don't know what to think of yourself? What do you believe about yourself when all your life you have been put down or compared to others? You may be well aware of what others think of you, but no one could know you fully because you don't even know yourself. You can never hope to become a Woman of Destiny until you recognize that you are God-Produced.

BEGINNING THE JOURNEY TO DESTINY

Allow me to be the first to admit that Cynthia's journey sounds an awful lot like my own. Perhaps it sounds amazingly similar to your own. You've searched for an understanding of yourself based on your family, friends, career, networks, economic status, etc. However you now realize that those paths have never been able to lead you to an awakening of who you really are. The only place to find such an answer is in your creator. In the book of Genesis, chapter one verses twenty-six through twenty-eight we are provided with an accounting of the creation of humankind. It is the first of two creation stories found in Genesis; the other is Genesis chapter two verses twenty-one through twenty-three.

Nestled in this first creation story we discover the formula for becoming a *"Woman of Destiny."* **If we ever hope to become "Women of Destiny" the first thing we must do is recognize that we are God-Produced.** Verse twenty-six reads, And God said, "Let us make man in our image, in our likeness." Genesis 1:26a (NIV)

In the "a" part of verse twenty-six we discover that we are not here by chance or some cosmic reaction in the earth. We are here because God conceived of us and went about a detailed creative process to bring us into being. Ladies, we must understand the importance of claiming God as our creator and knowing who this God of creation is, if we ever hope to become *"Women of Destiny."*

THE IMAGEO DEI
(THE IMAGE OF GOD)

To produce something, means to give being, form, or shape. When a seamstress wants to make something the first thing she uses is a pattern. The pattern is the blueprint for the outfit she wants to make. The pattern guides and governs the outcome of that which she seeks to create. When God produced us, God used a very interesting pattern. Here in this text we discover that God uses God's self as the pattern for creating woman.

In order for you to fully grasp the significance of this you must understand who God is. Without argument we can say that God is perfection, God is the material and spiritual manifestation of all that is good, God is joy, God is peace, God is love, God is wisdom, creativity, virtue, hope, and power. And therefore, when God created us in God's image and likeness, God created us with everything that is God. This means that everything you are - with your dark skin or light skin, long or short hair, small or round waist, full or thin lips, wide or skinny hips; you are divinely inspired, you are God's heavenly handiwork, you are a magnificent creation. You can be certain of this because of the image or pattern in which you were made. You must begin to recognize that in the fabric of your DNA, in the very blood that runs warm through your veins, in the wisdom residing in your mind, in the reflection that stares back from your mirror, there is God. It doesn't matter that you've been called - ugly, a mistake, stupid, worthless, a no body, or good for nothing. The "truth" is that you are God's finest creation, God's magnificent masterpiece, God's flawless formation, and God's glorious work of genius.

M. Scott Peck in his book the *"Road Less Traveled"* began with a profound one-line assertion. He said, "Life is difficult." He was indeed correct in his assertion. Life will try you, relationships will end, friends will stab you in your back, children will disappoint you, jobs will downsize, you will make mistakes, bill collectors will call, parents will get sick, and diseases will invade your body. But you must never forget that you are God-Produced and this ultimately means that you are more than a conqueror! When we recognize that we are made in God's image even our perceived problems and flaws become a part of the perfecting of our being. Romans chapter eight and verse twenty-eight says it best when it says, "And we know that all things work together for good to them that love God, to them who are called according to his purpose."

OUR PAST PREPARES US FOR OUR FUTURE

The greatest danger for African American women in particular and all women in general is that we forge into our tomorrows without understanding our yesterdays. Much of what we are experiencing as a community at present is a direct result of our history. We must acknowledge that there is a void in the African American community among *some* adult women. It is the vacuous life of women being lived without self-awareness. It is a life marked by a history of low self-esteem, self-hatred, self-abuse, denial, promiscuity, drug and alcohol abuse, and a complete lack of self-knowledge. For some, the African American woman is one to be objectified, dominated, abused, abandoned, scrutinized, labeled and left out. However, these descriptors emanate from and have their origin in the history of an enslaved people. Kelly Brown Douglas in her book, *"Sexuality and the Black Church"* explores the notion that "since women in general were held in such low regard by White patriarchal society, it is a logical conclusion for this culture to blame Black women for Black depravity."[1] Here we find Black women being used as the scapegoats for all that is immoral and corrupt in the Black community. Unfortunately, many African American women have chosen to believe this lie and therefore live beneath their promise and potential because they fail to recognize in whose image they are made. We must realize that we have carried our race on our backs for hundreds, yes even thousands of years and our race wouldn't be where it is without us. Genesis chapter one verse thirty-one goes on to say, *"God saw everything that God had made, and indeed, it was very good."* There is absolutely nothing that a woman could do to eradicate the goodness in her creation. Patricia Hunter states in her work *Women's Power - Women's Passion,* "If all God creates was very good, including humankind, then all women, regardless of ethnicity, class, varying abilities … are a part of God's very good creation. It is therefore our job to not only see the good in ourselves but to see it in others."[2]

WHAT YOU DON'T KNOW CAN HURT YOU

Before we can move on we must first take a look back to examine how a lack of self-knowledge has negatively affected our lives. Just think about the number of times you doubted yourself. Now think about the number of times you quit because you felt powerless. Finally, reflect on the number of times you made bad choices and indulged in self-destructive behavior because you were uncertain of yourself. Not knowing who you are can not only hurt you, it can destroy you.

African American women comprise the fastest growing population of persons being infected with HIV (Human Immunodeficiency Virus). Many have attributed this epidemic in our community to Black men being on the "Down Low." By this it is meant that there are Black men, who are married to, or dating Black women, while secretly having sex with other men, thusly infecting our women. Perhaps this is true and undoubtedly it is tragic. It is true that a woman's intuition is her greatest gift. And the truth is that most women know that there spouse or lover is bi-sexual. But what is it that makes us stay in that terminal, and toxic relationship? What causes us to turn our heads the other way and live in our comfortable houses of denial? What keeps us from knowing self and disables us from teaching our daughters to behave differently? What is it that keeps this cycle of abuse alive in our communities? Along with Down Low men we have Low Down women in our community. Women who mask their insecurity by engaging in shallow sexual relations with coupled and single men. We, African American women, must examine the root cause of our promiscuity and our pain. To continue to excuse our behavior by pointing the finger at others is futile.

I'm certain that there are many answers to the relationship psychosis suffered by so many in our community. However, I believe that much of it stems from the "Absentee Father" which leads to a lack of self-esteem and low self-concept. Allow me to explain. When your father is missing from childhood through adolescence to adulthood, you are left forever searching for that missing love. A father accepts a daughter in a way that no other person can or will (hence we get "Daddy's Girl"). A father will work night and day, forsaking himself to meet the needs of his daughter. A true father will give his life to defend his daughter and provide for not only her needs but also her wants. No one can hold a daughter in his arms and make her feel protected like Daddy. So what happens when Daddy is missing? Or what happens when Daddy was abusive or neglectful? Unfortunately, in every future relationship you enter into you look for that which Daddy didn't give. Chances are that you will allow your spouse or partner to abuse you verbally, physically, or emotionally because you long desperately for that Daddy approval that never comes. This same destructive behavior can emanate from a missing mother. When you finally awaken from the abyss you've created for yourself, you realize that you have been a co-conspirator in your own demise.

It is our job to look seriously at the pathology that is caused by not knowing who we are. Promiscuity is but one of the many destructive behaviors that we as women find ourselves engaging in when there is a lack of self-knowledge. Sex, because it is such a close and personal encounter, temporarily fills a void in us until the memory fades. We feel special, loved, wanted and needed until we realize that this was just another chance encounter ended. Before we know it, we are caught up in a cycle of promiscuity and not knowing how truly special we are has once again hurt us.

There are still other affects of not knowing oneself. We can become manipulators (needing to control everything and everyone around us in order to feel balanced or stable), haters (persons who are jealous of other's accomplishments because they lack their own), abusers (individuals who turn their negative inner feelings into negative outward behaviors on others or themselves to fill a void), addicts (persons who over-indulge in behaviors such as shopping, eating, alcohol, drugs, and sex to comfort their pain), etc. But, I am convinced that once you know whose image and likeness you are made in, you will be well on your way to becoming a "Woman of Destiny." Once you begin to walk in the realization of who you are, you can walk in the assurance that God has a wonderful plan for your life. You can hold your head up high and affirm your sisters and celebrate the plan that God is unfolding in their lives.

ONCE YOU KNOW WHO YOU ARE THINGS CHANGE

It has been said that opportunity favors those who are prepared. This is just another way of saying that doors will begin to open in your life when you stand ready to walk through them. These doors, ironically, were always there available for you to take full advantage of, however you were either blind to their presence, sitting in mediocrity unable to walk through, or afraid of your ability to handle the blessings on the other side. God has some doors ready and available for you to walk through today, however you must decide that you will believe enough in yourself to walk through those doors when they are presented to you.

Growing up in America in the late sixties and early seventies wasn't easy. I was a very dark-skinned little girl in a society that only accepted as beautiful and worthy those with white or light skin. I was constantly ridiculed and made fun of by not only other children in the neighborhood, but also my siblings. Everyone I saw on television that was considered beautiful was white or a very light-skinned Black person. I felt tortured and punished for being in this dark skin that God had given me, so I ran for refuge to the only person I thought could help me - Momma. My mother would routinely stop my brothers from teasing me but she couldn't always be there. So she did something so ingenious that I have never forgotten it. My mother sat me down in the kitchen one day after I had been crying from a barrage of verbal attacks by my brothers and she said to me "Sweetheart, you are the most beautiful girl in the whole wide world." I couldn't believe that she was saying this to me - didn't she have eyes - couldn't she see all the pretty girls on television and in the magazines? She lifted my little face up in the palm of her hands and she said beauty is in the eye of the beholder, and to me you are the most beautiful little girl in the whole wide world. Well, my mother had never lied to me before so why would she start now? Perhaps there was some truth to what she was saying and I should never be ashamed of this wonderful skin I was in. I began to walk with confidence, smile more, assert my personality, make more friends, and care more for my appearance. Little did I recognize that as soon as I started believing in myself, others would do the same. This was the start of something monumental in my life. I had figured out a great and wise truth that is hidden from so many people but is able to set them free. *I discovered that what you believe about yourself - either good or bad - can free you or incarcerate you.* I realized that your attitude really does determine your altitude. I believe that my mother understood that I was made in the image of God. If only more mothers could instill in their daughters what my mother instilled in me that day, we would have less prostitution, less drug addiction, and less self-hatred. I would have more days of doubting myself, but I could always hear my mother's voice somewhere in the faint distance saying, "You are the most beautiful little girl in the whole wide world." To rephrase the Bible, "As a woman thinketh so is she." I've discovered that we truly are what we think.

Remember these words, "You are made in the image of Almighty God, and regardless of what you have endured in your life you are more than a conqueror." If you can embrace these truths in your heart there is no goal too great, no task too difficult, and no obstacle too overbearing. Your task for this day and every day is to see yourself as complete, whole, powerful, smart, ambitious, and unafraid. Because you are made in the image of God you are a "Woman of Destiny" and great things are in store for you. Know that there are other great women who have embraced this truth of being God-Produced and they have blazed a trail before you. Think about Mary McLeod Bethune and her tenacity in building one of the first institutions of higher education for African Americans. Think about Oprah Winfrey and how she was able to overcome her childhood of abandonment, sexual abuse and poverty to become the most powerful woman in media. You are made in the image of God and therefore God is able to do even greater works through you.

[1] Kelly Brown Douglas, Sexuality and the Black Church, (Maryknoll, New York: Orbis Books, 1999), 35.

[2] Patricia L. Hunter. "Women's Power -Women's Passion: And God Said, "That's Good"." A Troubling in my Soul: Womanist Perspectives on Evil and Suffering, edited by Emilie M. Townes. New York: Orbis Books, 1993. p. 189-190.

GROWTH THROUGH CONTEMPLATION
"WHO AM I?"

1. Do you ever struggle with understanding who you really are?

2. Do you feel that you are made in the image and likeness of God?

3. If so, what qualities or characteristics of God do you believe you possess?

4. What qualities or characteristics of God do you feel you are lacking?

5. Describe the qualities/characteristics that society has placed upon you as a woman.

6. Which of these qualities can you agree with and which ones do you disagree with?

7. As you reflect on your life, what struggles have you encountered because of lack of self-knowledge (e.g., low self-esteem, promiscuity, self-hatred, denial, addictions, etc.)?

8. How can understanding yourself as being God-Produced help you in beginning the process of overcoming these struggles?

CHAPTER TWO

God –
POSITIONED

"And God said, Let us make man in our image, in our likeness: and let *them* rule over the fish of the sea and the birds of the air, over the livestock, over all the earth, and over all the creatures that move along the ground."
GENESIS 1: 26 (NIV)

I t was a week before Christmas when all the senior associates gathered in the staff conference room for the big announcement. Karen could feel her knees trembling, her heart pounding and her hands sweating as she and the others waited to hear who would be the new Vice President of Marketing and Sales. Her mind began to slowly wander as she reminisced of her childhood. She recalled standing in the crowd of neighborhood kids waiting for her name to be called for the next team and inwardly reflecting, "Why do girls always finish last?" Growing up with only brothers as mentors Karen became what we refer to as a "tomboy." She caught a football like a NFL wide receiver and was the only girl in the neighborhood who could dunk a basketball on the homemade court. Pretty dresses, make-up and dolls didn't thrill her; they were all signs of weakness in her eyes. When Christmas rolled around she was happiest with action toys or bicycles that would allow her to keep up with the boys. She was forced to fight for everything growing up. She fought to be heard in a room full of boys, she fought for food at the dinner table, she fought verbally and physically to keep from being the family punching bag. She was the girl that boys were afraid of and she relished the reputation as the one girl you didn't want to mess with. She carried that same mentality into high school and boys became best friends, not boyfriends. Some members of her family even became concerned that perhaps she was a lesbian because she didn't run after the boys, as did the other high school girls; she was more interested in running with the boys. You see Karen believed that boys possessed all the power while girls struggled to gain position. She vowed to herself that she would do everything in her power to keep up with and surpass the boys. All of her life she thought the fighting was meant to kill her, but now she realized it had only made her stronger. So, she drove a sports car, she lived in a bachelorette pad, she never allowed herself to be in a truly loving relationship, and she treated education as a means of getting ahead. Karen was what many considered hard, cold and callous. But she viewed herself as focused, unyielding and strong.

Karen decided that she would do anything not to be thought of as weak or powerless and therefore she became an over-achiever. What she didn't realize however, was that she didn't have to abandon who she was to achieve something she already had (equality). As clapping broke through her momentary daydreaming, she realized that the position had been given to Jennifer. It was then that Karen realized her struggle to prove her equality had cost her years of not knowing and celebrating herself. She vowed on that day to stop trying to be like the boys and start being the beautiful, self-assured, intelligent woman that God had created her to be.

NOW THAT I KNOW WHO I AM, TELL ME WHERE I STAND

As we continue on this journey toward self-discovery and spiritual self-actualization, we must recognize that we are not only God-Produced, but secondly we must recognize that we are God-Positioned. After God fashions man and woman in God's image and after God's likeness, the Bible says that God speaks and says "let *them* rule over." Here we discover God establishing a very valid and factual principle of *equity* amongst the sexes. That's right I said equity, and it's not a dirty word. When God speaks and says, "Let *them* rule over," God is saying I want the man and woman to have supreme authority, power and say so over all the earth. Unfortunately, our patriarchal society has for centuries instructed humanity that the woman is inferior to the man. The Christian church has jumped on the bandwagon and embraced this sexist mindset and used Genesis chapter three verse sixteen to create a false hierarchy. In that scripture it says, *"The woman's desire shall be to her husband and he shall <u>rule</u> over her."* Now in order to fully understand this scripture one must first put it in its proper perspective or context. When God passed down this edict it was after humans had committed sin, disobeyed God, and chosen to follow their own willful ways. God therefore spoke these words as a judgment against humanity. When we embrace an understanding of men on top and women on the bottom or a "hierarchy of existence", we must recognize that this was never God's original intent for humanity. And the truth is while pulpiteers recognize that Jesus came as the second Adam to correct the fall and pay for the sins of humankind, many have chosen to subjugate women and relegate them to certain places in the church and society by using this scripture. My mentor and friend, Dr. John W. Kinney says that they continue to operate under a fallen theology, that he coined, "Snakeology." It is the theology of the snake that predicates itself on humans needing to have something outside of them to be powerful. Thus we find Adam and Eve eating the forbidden fruit and today we find ourselves indulging in all manner of addictions and sins searching for happiness. It is a theology based upon the fall and not upon the redemption that Christ brings. When Christ died on Calvary he paid the penalty for our sins, thus returning us to our original glory and authority. God never intended for us to be in competition with one another, or beholding to one another, or feeling inferior or afraid of one another. The truth of creation is that we were created to be *equal* and in *partnership*. When God created us there were no "Big I's" and "little u's". Therefore, we are all precious in the sight of God and in order to become "Women of Destiny" we must resume our rightful place in this world.

Allow me to illuminate my point by providing you with a life story. In 1821, on a slave-breeding plantation in Maryland, a female child was born to Harriet and Benjamin Ross. Although she was born at what we call the bottom of the rung, a slave, black and female, she grew up to become the most famous of all the conductors on the Underground Railroad. She has been described as a big-souled, God-intoxicated, heroic Black woman. You see many people only know Harriet Tubman as the Black Moses who risked her life 19 times to bring more than 300 slaves to freedom, but what they don't know is that she was the only woman to have led U.S. Army troops in battle during the Civil War. What am I trying to get you to see? Harriet Tubman was able to do what she did because she decided that the fight for freedom wasn't just a man's job. She realized that God had *positioned* her such that she could do what no other *person* could do.

I'm not certain what woman is reading the words of this book and feeling as if she has been relegated to a certain station in life.

Perhaps you've hit the glass ceiling and there's no where left for you to go at your company. Well, start your own company. Maybe you're in a relationship where you're afraid to voice your opinion. Well begin to speak up, it's your God-ordained right and if you're still not heard, move on to a place where you can be heard and valued. You are God-Positioned, which means that you have been given rule over; that means control, power, authority, and say-so over all the earth. If you are going to be a "Woman of Destiny" you're going to have to stand up and take your rightful place - beside and not behind - next to and not under. Ladies, God didn't create you as the tail, you weren't an afterthought; you are an important player in this game called life. The church wouldn't be what it is without women. Your job wouldn't be what it is without women. Your family certainly wouldn't be what it is without women. Therefore, the world wouldn't be what it is without women. Women can do anything they put their minds to because we have been given authority. Whenever you begin to get discouraged, just remember that Jesus had so much faith and belief in the ability of women that he entrusted them to be the first to carry the Gospel message. In Matthew's gospel chapter twenty-eight verses eight through ten, it is recorded that after an angel had encountered Mary Magdalene and Mary the mother of Jesus at the tomb and informed them of Jesus' ascension the women hurried away to tell the disciples. It was then that Jesus met them while they were still filled with mixed emotions of joy and fear to reassure them that he had indeed risen. He thought enough of women to entrust them with the good news that death had not spoken the final word and that he would see his disciples again. The Bible says in Philippians chapter four and verse thirteen, "I can do all things through Christ who strengthens me." That simply means that because of the shed blood of Jesus I have been reconciled to my former state of being; a being that was created to have authority over all the earth.

THE PROBLEM WITH RE-POSITIONING

If this chapter makes re-positioning and taking your rightful place in this world sound easy, I do apologize. Re-establishing your God-given place in this world is extremely difficult. It is arduous, mainly because of the patriarchal system in which we live. This system was designed and structured to give men the advantage over women in the workplace, the political arena, the home, the church, the community and any other place you can think of. From the boardroom to the bedroom women continually struggle to be recognized, appreciated, valued, respected, and honored. It is a struggle as old as time itself and one that deeply permeates the Bible. The historical context in which the Bible was written was one in which men played a dominant role in all the aforementioned areas. It is for this reason that many of the oppressive statements made by Paul in the New Testament were and continue to be widely accepted.

So the question is asked, "How then do I reclaim my position in the world?" I answer, "with longsuffering or patience and much prayer." Patriarchy, like many other systems of oppression, benefits greatly those who currently hold power within that system. Power is never easily surrendered, even if it is only perceived. Therefore women must be shrewd, tactful, bold, and yet gentle. Matthew chapter ten verse sixteen finds Jesus instructing his disciples saying, "Behold, I send you forth as a sheep in the midst of wolves, be ye therefore wise as serpents, and harmless as doves." By no means do I want to suggest that men are wolves; however, women must learn to navigate this wolverine system of patriarchy with the savvy of a serpent and the gentleness of a dove. We must also be willing to suffer the consequences like the women in our past who have made great strides. We must be intelligent enough to recognize that doing nothing about the current atrocities against women is sending the message that we believe that everything is alright. We must be bold enough to risk losing our popularity when we go against the grain. We must be visionaries enough to see that we can positively change the direction of the world by taking our rightful place beside and not behind. We must be supportive enough to encourage our sisters who have begun making the necessary steps toward equality for humanity and our brothers who are partnering with us in the struggle.

You see the reason I am able to speak so passionately about this area is because I have journeyed down this path of God-Positioning. My story begins at the Howard University School of Divinity. It was there in 1989 that I found myself working on a Master of Divinity degree. On a particularly hot and humid day in Washington, I decided to visit one of my seminary professors to gain more insight from him on his recently published book. As I knocked on the door of Dr. Cain Hope Felder, I noticed that he was not alone. There were two other persons in his office, one was his daughter and the other was my future husband. As time progressed and the future unfolded itself, I found myself standing before the altar exchanging vows with my friend Lewis with Dr. Felder next to him as his best man. Not long after I was married, my husband began sharing with me that he never wanted to be married to a preacher. I was floored by this given that we met in seminary. What did he think I wanted to do with my life, become a nuclear physicist? Being what I thought was the perfect little *submissive* wife, I terminated my seminary studies and sat on my call for seven long years until the pain and constant jeering from God became too much. I wasn't sleeping because sermons were racing through my mind. I couldn't keep my thoughts off of ministry and what God required of me next. I was busy working in the church, helping my husband grow a new church start to over 500 members in four years. However, because of religious sexism I wasn't able to fully accept my call to ministry. Then it happened - enough became enough - I was sick and tired of being sick and tired. Knowing that discussing this matter with my husband would only lead to a heated argument, I sat down and wrote a four-page letter. In that letter I did something that I would never suggest any women do unless she is completely certain of her call. In that letter I gave my husband this ultimatum, "Either you accept that I am called to the ministry and support me or else I'm leaving. Please don't make me choose between you and God, because God will win!" My husband realized that I was serious and that God's "yes" was louder than his "no." He also realized that my call to ministry was as legitimate as his call to ministry. Two weeks later he recognized persons in the church who felt they had a call on their lives. I arose and walked to the altar for prayer. He put me up to preach my initial sermon three months later and the rest is history. It was my husband who encouraged me to go back and finish my seminary degree and he served as my greatest supporter as I completed my Doctorate degree. I could be bitter and dwell on the fact that I sat on my call for seven years, but in those seven years I had two beautiful children, gained a wealth of experience in the fields of psychology, education and religion, and discovered what I was made of.

Now that I am an ordained minister of the gospel my husband and I share in team ministry. He often remarks that he feels blessed because he can count on me in so many ways. He can leave the church and know that the people are in good hands with me. We share the preaching, teaching, administration, counseling and other responsibilities of the church. Truly I cannot imagine what my life would be like if I hadn't taken that bold step toward re-positioning to get in line with what God had intended for my life. The question is asked, "Was it easy?" The answer is, "Absolutely not!" This has been a journey for both my husband and I - a journey of acceptance, a journey of checking our egos, a journey of recognizing and celebrating one another's gifts, a journey of tears, a journey of laughter, but all in all a journey of love.

Ladies, it is not until you recognize that you were made to be equal with all humanity - regardless of sex, age, class, race, physical disability, etc., that you can become a "Woman of Destiny." Once I embraced this great truth for my life I began to see doors of opportunity open for me in my career, education, personal life, and finances. My mother used to say, "It's a sorry dog that won't wag its own tail." In so many words she was saying that at some point in your life you must recognize who you are and where you stand and be ready to let someone else know the same. Women will never know equality until they begin to claim it for themselves. You must remember that power concedes to nothing but power. If you ever hope to reach your highest heights you must recognize your God given position and authority in the world and use it. Mark my words, opportunities will avail themselves to you as soon as you begin to believe that no opportunity is too great for you!

GROWTH THROUGH CONTEMPLATION
"WHERE DO I STAND?"

1. Have you ever felt inferior to your male counterparts? Why or why not?

2. What do you believe God meant when he said *"And let them rule over?"*

3. What makes you feel uncomfortable about proclaiming equality with your male counterparts?

4. Do you truly believe that Jesus came to restore humanity through the shedding of his blood? If so, what does this say about sexism and classism?

5. What are some of your personal struggles brought on by a hierarchical system (ex. Inability to be promoted on the job, relegated to "women's work" in the church)?

6. What or who do you believe to be your greatest obstacle in achieving your rightful place in the world?

7. If you were given the opportunity tomorrow what would you do, or be that is being hindered by our current system of inequality?

8. As you reflect on your life, what issues have you developed because of your perceived position in the world (e.g., objectification, low self-esteem, self-hatred, denial, addictions, etc.)?

9. How has understanding yourself as being God-Positioned helped you in beginning the process of overcoming these issues?

CHAPTER THREE

God–
PARTNERED

"And Ruth said intreat me not to leave thee, or to return from following after thee: for wither thou goest, I will go; and where thou lodgest, I will lodge: thy people shall be my people, and thy God my God."

RUTH 1:16 (KJV)

Toni and Lynn had been best friends since their freshman year in high school. It seemed then that they both possessed the appropriate awkwardness and insecurity that made them inseparable in their search for recognition. Toni was ambitious, smart, determined but completely self-conscious. Lynn on the other hand was beautiful, graceful and able to turn heads just by entering a room. After high school graduation they both attended the same college and there seemed to be nothing that could separate them. Lynn was always the one with boyfriends while Toni was more interested in getting to the library and making the grade. When Toni did finally stumble into a relationship she excitedly shared her good news with her best friend only to discover that Lynn wasn't as excited. "How do you know you really love him?" Lynn asked pointedly. "Because I know what love feels like," barked Toni. "But how would you know when you never really had any boyfriends in high school?" Lynn sarcastically responded. Toni replied, "Just because you've had more boyfriends than me doesn't mean you are the only one who can recognize love." Suddenly it hit Toni that Lynn would never be excited about her new relationship because it meant that Toni had it all - great parents, a wonderful apartment, a paid off car, a degree, a successful career and now a man. While Lynn had a great boyfriend she was still struggling to get her college degree. Now some fourteen years after they first became friends, Toni wondered if Lynn would even show up for her wedding. Something happened in those years that tragically separated friend from friend. "That's it", Toni thought to herself, "I'm finished with girlfriends. Who needs them anyway?"

UNDERSTANDING RELATIONSHIPS

Why did God create us to need others? I sometimes think it would have been so much easier if God could have simply created us in such a way that relationships could be optional. In this way, persons who wanted relationships could have them and be happy and those who didn't could be content alone. The truth is, this was not God's design for humanity. God created us in such a way that we are born with a need to be in relationship with one another from birth. Babies who are neglected at birth and not held are at a greater risk of dying than those who are held and loved. Just as we need food and shelter for our bodies to survive, we also need relationships for our souls to survive. If we fail to cultivate meaningful, whole relationships with God and with one another we run the risk of spiritually dying. When God created man in the garden, he noticed that he was the only one in creation without a counterpart. In Genesis chapter two and verse eighteen God speaks and says, *"It is not good that the man should be alone..."* Here God was making a foundational case for humanity to recognize the importance and necessity for relationships.

If you ever hope to become a "Woman of Destiny" you must not only recognize that you are God-Produced and know that you are God-Positioned, you must be willing to be God-Partnered. In other words you must be willing to develop intimate relationships such as sista girlfriends, mentoring relationships, parenting relationships, marriages and friendships with others that will ultimately enhance your ability to live out your purpose. This is not optional! Remember, *"No woman is an island and no woman stands alone!"*

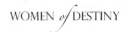

THE PROBLEM

You see I truly believe that women could rule the world. I believe that women could run this country and other countries (if Bush and Blair can do it, so can we). We could certainly balance the nation's budget, our ability to balance our household budgets with little money and great responsibility is a tangible qualification. We could run major corporations. We already run our families, our neighborhoods, the little league team, our sorority and the church ministry, all at once. We could create opportunities for our children to be well educated and prepared to face the rigors of the world. We can keep our men happy, our friends entertained, our children focused, our co-workers on task and our churches filled. I believe we can do anything we put our minds to doing. But, I also believe that there is one thing standing in the way of our success; one dilemma, one stumbling block, one hurdle, and that problem is - we just can't seem to get along. We dislike one another for no good reason. I'm certain that you've heard this comment - "I just don't like her!" We dislike one another because deep down we are envious of what another sister has. We talk about each other and assassinate one another's character because at the core of it all we don't like ourselves. We try to steal one another's husband or boyfriend and cause division in each other's homes because we've never felt loved and now we are so desperate we will do anything to hear those three words, "I love you!" Women could rule the world, but the simple reality that we can't get along, gets in our way. It's time for us to deal with our foolishness because the truth is we need each other. Ladies, I'm calling a time out. We need to get over to the bench so we can discuss our ridiculous behavior on the court of life, that's seriously causing us to lose the game. I don't know about you, but I'm not only trying to make it to the playoffs, I'm trying to win the championship.

THE SOLUTION

In order for us to spiritually self-actualize we must learn how to be in relationship. I'm not speaking of any kind of relationship, but relationships that are built on a firm Godly foundation. In order to truly embrace an understanding of what kind of relationship God wants for us, let us look at the story of Naomi and Ruth. In the first chapter of the book of Ruth we discover two women on the way to their destiny. The story of Naomi and Ruth, mother and daughter-in-law, provide us with the necessary ingredients for God-Partners. (These partnerships can be with husband, boyfriend, sista-girlfriends, mentor, etc.). In the story of Naomi and Ruth we find a mother-in-law (Naomi) and her daughter-in-law (Ruth) in a very desperate situation. Naomi has become widowed and her two sons (Mahlon and Chilion) have died. Naomi decides to return to her homeland and therefore she begins to bid her farewells. She tells her two daughters-in-law (Ruth and Orpah) that they should return to their mothers while she returns to her home town of Bethlehem.

In that sixteenth verse of chapter one, we discover God's creation of a true God friendship when Ruth makes a passionate appeal to Naomi. Try to picture it - Ruth down on one knee, tears streaming from her reddened eyes, her right fist clutching the dress of Naomi while her left fist clutches a handful of dirt as she strains to put her passion into words. Barely able to speak, she takes a deep breath and says, "Don't ask me to leave you! Let me go with you. Wherever you go, I will go." Let's pause right here. Ladies, if we ever hope to reach our destination in God the first thing we must do is develop relationships that are going in the *right direction.* The people around you serve as the compass for your life. If they are going in the wrong direction, it won't be long before you discover that you are also going in the wrong direction. But, if they are going in the right direction you can be certain that you are headed for your Promised Land. Ruth knew that Naomi was a woman that she could trust to be moving in the right direction. Naomi had a track record with Ruth that proved she was a woman of God; she had proven she was strong, she could run her household, and she loved her family. She was a woman who was about something.

Take a quick moment and evaluate your friendships. Think about the people you hang with, your girls, your partners, and your lovers, and ask yourself the question, "Are these people headed in the right direction?" Not because they drive a nice car, wear nice clothes, belong to the right social clubs, know the right people, or live in a big house, but because they know God and their purpose in life! Listen, your friends must be people who know where they are going. If not, it will be like the blind leading the blind. And the truth is, many of us are being led by blind women and men right now. If you could be honest for one moment, you would have to admit that most of your relationships are like aimless rides on a merry-go-round. Sometimes they're up, sometimes they're down but most of the time they're just going around and around and never getting anywhere. No direction! God wants you to be in God partnerships that are helping you to move into your promise; relationships that are focused on Godly fellowship (not Friday night happy hour); relationships that include prayer (and not just partying); relationships that talk about the Good News (and not the latest gossip). Ruth said in so many words, "Naomi wherever you go, count me in. I'm dedicated to following you because I know you're moving in the right direction." My father-in-law, the late Bishop Lewis Tait, Sr., used to say, "If you don't know where you're going, any road will get you there". What road do your friends, lovers and associates have you on today? Are you on the road to pain or power, the road to turmoil or triumph, the road to victimization or victory, the road to sin or salvation, the road to blindness or blessings, the road to depression or deliverance, the road to hell or heaven. Ask yourself, "Are my friends headed in the right direction and if not, how long will I continue to follow them?"

We must first develop friendships that are moving in the right direction. Secondly, this text teaches us that we must develop friendships that lead to the right *destination*. In the text Ruth says, "Don't ask me to leave you! Let me go with you. Wherever you go, I will go; *wherever you live, I will live.*" To live means to establish one's self, settle down, make a home, and create a destiny. Dianna Ross put it like this, "Do you know where you're going to, do you like the things that life is showing you, where are you going to, do you know?" "Women of Destiny" must align themselves, as Ruth did, with friends who know their destination. Women, like Naomi, who know what they want out of life. These are women who aren't afraid to make mistakes along the journey because they know that God has ordered their steps and secured their futures. This is such a simple and practical truth; you would think that everyone would get it. If you wanted to be a scholar why follow after a dropout, if you want to be financially independent why follow someone who is building debt instead of building wealth, if you want to be happy why hang around with miserable people, if you want to be drug-free why spend time around addicts, if you want to be Godly why follow an atheist. You see if more parents took the time to teach their children this lesson we would have happier homes. If more supervisors taught this to their employees we would have more productive workplaces. If more preachers taught this to their congregations we would have more powerful churches. Come on, you would never go on a trip without knowing the destination, how long it's going to take, how far it is, where your final destination will be, where you will stop along the way, and how long you plan on staying there. So why do you and your friends move through life so aimlessly without a destination, a goal, or a dream. Determine on today that you will have friends who are not only moving in the right direction but who also know their destination.

We know that we need to surround ourselves with people who are moving in the right direction and who know their destination. Now the third thing we must do is align ourselves with friends who have the right *associations.* Ruth in that sixteenth verse goes on to say, *"Your people will be my people."* In order to fully grasp the significance of this statement we must have an understanding of the importance of tribal associations. Naomi (the mother-in-law) was from the tribe of Judah in the village of Bethlehem. She was from a tribe that served Yahweh. Her people had experienced the awesomeness of Yahweh as he freed them from Egyptian bondage and led them into the Promised Land. Naomi was from the town that would serve as the birthplace of the Savior of the world. Ruth, however, was from the Moabite tribe of the pagan nation called Moab. The Moabite nation had a different history. It began with the incestuous relationship between Lot and his elder daughter depicted in Genesis chapter nineteen and verse thirty-six. The Moabites were perpetual enemies of Israel. And so here we find Ruth attempting to unite with Naomi and her people. Ruth is willing to give up her past associations (or history) to embrace Naomi's associations and culture. What am I trying to get you to see? God wants us to have friendships that will bring us into association with the right people. These are people of high morals and values and spiritual understanding. God wants us to be associated with persons who will force us to give up those beliefs, habits, behaviors, and lifestyles that are leading to our destruction (i.e., smoking, drinking, sexing, hanging, cheating, lying, and stealing). Understand ladies that if your relationships aren't hooking you up or associating you with people whose lives speak to the promise, possibility, and power of God, you need to let them go. If you associate with un-Godly people long enough they will have you believing a lie is the truth and the truth is a lie. They'll tell you, "You can have a little smoke as long as it's not hard drugs. You can go out with a married man as long as the wife doesn't find out. It's alright to lie if it doesn't hurt anybody. You can keep the tithe as long as God knows your heart. You don't need to go to Bible study if you've been in the church over two years. Even if you're an alcoholic you can have a drink as long as you don't get too drunk. It's alright to shack up if you love each other because no one else is looking. You don't have to serve in the church if you don't want to." But these are all untruths and they are spread the same way Satan tempted Eve in the Garden of Eden; "Did God really say that you couldn't eat of that tree?"

If your associations aren't *elevating* you, they are *destroying* you. Ruth followed Naomi because she knew her people were people she could associate with.

In other words, if you are going to be a "Woman of Destiny" you must stop trying to fit in with the wrong people. The Bible says in Titus chapter two and verse fourteen that, *"Jesus gave himself for us, that he might redeem us from all iniquity, and purify unto himself a peculiar people."* The reason you don't fit in with the crowd at work is because you're not supposed to, you're a peculiar person. Your family isn't supposed to understand you, everybody isn't going to like you, and the popular people will reject you, because you are a peculiar person. Say it out loud to yourself, "I'm peculiar!" Now say it with some pride. "I'm peculiar!" You see this means you've got to find other peculiar people to hang with, talk with, pray with, live with, go to school with, and work with.

First, you must find friends that are going in the right *direction;* secondly they must know their *destination,* thirdly they must have the right *associations*. Fourth and finally, you must have friendships with the proper **dedication**. Let's examine verse sixteen. It reads, *"Don't ask me to leave! Let me go with you. Wherever you go, I will go; wherever you live I will live. Your people will be my people, and your **God** will be my **God**."* Ruth was from a religious heritage that acknowledged God with the impersonal name of Elohim. Naomi's tradition knew God as Yahweh, which intimated a close personal relationship. Remember, Ruth was a Moabite while Naomi was an Israelite. Ruth didn't know God on a close intimate basis like Naomi. So when Ruth makes this pronouncement, she is saying in essence I want to *dedicate* myself to your God. From this day forward your God will be my God. She was devoting herself to following and learning about this God, praying to this God, and worshipping this God. If we ever hope to reach our potential in God, our relationships, like this relationship between Ruth and Naomi, must be grounded in our dedication to God. Listen ladies, time is winding up, "Women of Destiny" must begin to bond with other Christian women and men in order for us to win this world for Christ. We must get to the place where we can count on one another to be dedicated. You see I need to know that when times get rough and hell hounds are on my trail, I've got some friends I can call to stand in the gap. I've got some prayer warriors who know the power of prayer. I'm not interested in hanging out at the club with my girlfriends, waiting to pick up somebody who won't even remember my name the next day. I'm interested in friends who like to hang out in the house of God and worship God, bless the Lord, exalt God's name, and give God the praise.

A TESTIMONY FROM
A RECOVERING SISTER-HATER

Allow me to share my own story because I am a recovering sista-hater. I grew up with two older brothers and no sisters. I always found it easier to talk to boys and hang out with the fellas. Whenever I tried to make friends with the sisters, there always seemed to be some drama, hatred, man stealing, gossiping and confusion. I completely gave up on befriending women because it was just too much trouble.

Stephen Spielberg directed Alice Walker's *"The Color Purple"* in 1985 and through this big screen production my life was changed. As I watched the various female-to-female relationships that existed in this movie, I realized that while the dysfunction was great, our need for these relationships is greater. The film portrayed everything from undying love between sisters, to hurtful friendships, to genuine care and concern. Through this movie God pricked my heart and showed me that I needed female friends, just not the ones I had been choosing. So I started praying because I had dealt with enough foolishness with women in my life. I prayed and I asked God to send me some God-fearing, self-assured, principled, about the business sista-girlfriends. God answered my prayer and I've never been happier. I've discovered that there are sisters in this world with similar dreams and aspirations for the kingdom. I've discovered that there are women who will pray for you and not prey on you. I've discovered that male friends are wonderful and husbands are the best, but there is nothing like having a sista-girlfriend to share your secrets, fears, pains and hang-ups with. I'm certain that there is some woman reading this book even now who, like me, had given up on being friends with women, but I appeal to you today to hang in there because Godly sista-girlfriends are worth the struggle.

Allow me to also speak to the women who are reading this book and now recognize that your relationships are toxic. You know a relationship is toxic and not God-partnered when you argue all the time, have to walk on eggshells and watch your every word because the friend might lose it, you hide other friendships because of jealousy, or share only some of your accomplishments because of haseration. When you discover that you are in one of these types of relationships you must, as painful as it is, end it. Whenever we remain in dysfunctional friendships we enable people to remain sick. It's important that we not be martyrs suffering to save toxic friends because "it's the right thing to do". Love is unconditional, but love does not require us to kill ourselves in service to another. The best we can do is support our toxic partners by giving them space to learn from our example as we step into our destiny. At some point, when everyone moves away from a person, they will realize that there must be something wrong with their behavior and hopefully they will get the necessary help.

As "Women of Destiny" we must find friends that are going in the right *direction*, know their *destination*, and have the right *associations*, with the proper *dedication*.

GROWTH THROUGH CONTEMPLATION
"WHO STANDS WITH ME?"

1. Do you believe that God created us to be in relationship or is this optional?

2. Is the husband the only person who can be a helpmeet (helper) to a woman?"

3. If you answered yes to #2, what does this say to single women who may never marry? Are they incomplete?

4. Do you believe that women have problems getting along with one another? What does it stem from?

5. How can women begin to heal the rift that exists between them?

6. What have been some of the problems that have resulted in your life from following people who were headed in the wrong direction?

7. How important is it that your friends know their destination in life? Why?

8. As a Christian, do you have a problem being referred to as "a peculiar person?" How should your friendships differ from a non-Christian?

9. How has not having God-Partnerships affected your life in the past?

CHAPTER FOUR

God-
PURPOSED

"So God created man in his own image, in the image of God he created him; male and female created he them. God blessed them and said to them, Be fruitful and (multiply) increase in number, fill the earth, and subdue it. Rule over the fish of the sea, and the birds of the air, and over every living thing that moves on the ground." GENESIS 1: 27-28 (NIV))

For years and years Patricia searched for the true meaning of her life. Everyday she awakened to the reality of spending eight to ten hours at a job she truly despised. Mondays were especially a chore because they highlighted the complete void and emptiness she would feel for four more days. Pat, as her friends called her, assumed this was the way life was to be lived. For as long as she could remember, it was drilled in her head by her parents, school teachers, Girl Scout leader, and Sunday school instructor, "You must follow the steps to success". She was obedient and so she got an education and experience, got a good job, was making money, and was still in search for the good husband, 2.5 children and a dog that would leave her happy and content. Patricia, like so many women, believed that her life would have meaning and purpose once she found a husband and had a few children. All her life she had been told that this was the answer to life's mystery of fulfillment and therefore it became her solution and primary goal. Patricia wasn't beautiful, by the world's standards, so she felt compelled to go the extra mile. She was always manicured, poised, polished, and prepared because any day could be the day she met Mr. Right. When she got married, she discovered that two wedding bands and a couple of "I do's" can't make you happy. Children soon followed and what a joy they were, but instead of pouring meaning and purpose into her life, she soon discovered that their job was to draw life from her like a Hoover vacuum attacking a dirty floor. So she wandered for years on end searching for meaning, but she was looking in all the wrong places. I'm not exactly certain when it happened, but one day the light came on. She realized in that instance that if she didn't find out her reason for being on this

earth, she would die a miserable woman. She would leave this earth never knowing passion, excitement, joy or peace. This meant she had to do something that I believe a lot of women find extremely difficult. She had to focus some attention on herself. She had to reserve some of her own time for the development of herself. She had to pull away from her husband, require him to share the load with the children and stop being a single parent in a two parent household. She began to read more. She spent quiet time alone with herself and with God. She discovered that the more time she committed to herself, the more joy she found. It was as if the light bulb went on and she understood why the flight attendant on the plane would tell the adults to put their oxygen mask on first in the case of an emergency and then attend to their children. They wanted people to understand that while you love your children, and are willing to sacrifice everything for them, if you don't tend to your needs first, you will die trying to meet their needs. And so she put on the proverbial oxygen mask and she took some long deep breaths until she surfaced a revived woman. That's when she knew she had a call on her life. She told her husband that God was requiring her heart, soul and mind - not in death but in life. Her husband supported her as she returned to school to become a Christian Counselor. She now owns and operates the largest Christian Counseling agency in the state of Pennsylvania. The last time we talked, she told me that her life has such inexplicable meaning and purpose, that she awakens everyday excited about the good she can do and about the blessings coming her way. But please understand that Patricia didn't stumble upon her purpose - it evaded her like a child playing hide and go seek - until one day she decided no more games, this is my life.

WHEN WHO I AM MEETS WHAT I DO

If we ever hope to become "Women of Destiny" we must begin the very difficult journey of self-discovery (God-Produced); finding our place in the world (God-Positioned); and finding others who will journey with us (God-Partnered). However the journey doesn't end there, you must also come to understand that you are God-Purposed. Verses twenty-seven and twenty-eight of the first chapter of Genesis provide us with our God-Purpose. If you've ever wondered, "What is my purpose?" "Why was I created?" "What am I here for?" these passages provide the prescription. In these verses God provides us with our "raison d'être" or our reason for being. God tells us we must be fruitful and multiply. In other words, God wants us to bring forth life, and then see to it that this process is duplicated. To be fruitful means to bear blessings, to be abundantly productive, and to yield a harvest. Our lives should be lived in such a manner that it is clear that we are positively affecting change in the lives of those around us. When the final scene of our lives has been acted out and the curtain of life closes on us, we should receive a standing ovation for all the sacrificial love and blessings we brought to this world. Our funerals should be full of people who are willing to testify that this woman was a blessing in my life. Someone else should jump up and excitedly proclaim, "If it had not been for this wonderful soul, I don't know where I would be." Take a moment and think about the people who have had this kind of positive impact on your life. It could have been a school teacher, mentor, parent, relative, classmate, or neighbor. These were the people who understood the principle of being fruitful.

Let me see if I can use an example to make this point crystal clear. Take a quick second to think of yourself as a fruit-bearing tree. You could choose an apple tree, pear tree, cherry tree or your favorite fruit tree. I like to think of myself as a beautiful, sprawling, orange tree that's planted by the rivers of water. My branches are strong, my roots go deep, my leaves are a vibrant green and my oranges are bright, beautiful and big. Now imagine that every large, beautifully formed, nutritious orange that grows from me is a result of using the God-given gifts and talents that I possess for others. Every orange is someone's life that I helped to transform. Every orange is some child I helped to educate. Every orange is some elderly person I stopped to love. Every orange is representative of the hope, love, and respect that I deposited in someone. Every orange is a soul that I led to Christ. You see, this is what God means by being fruitful. Women of Destiny know that they have a purpose to be *fruitful*. It doesn't matter how much money you have, what kind of car you drive, where you can send your children to school, what country clubs you belong to, or where you can shop. The only thing that matters in life is how much fruit you bear.

Many of us have become confused by our world system that rewards us on what it values. Therefore if you are a movie star, a business mogul, a famed author, a big time entertainer, or a famous sports figure you are lauded over by the world. The world makes a great big deal over you regardless of how many people you bless by your being. Christians must recognize however that there will come a day of reconciliation with God. We will stand before God and God will show us our fruit. Nothing that we have accomplished for ourselves will matter, not bank accounts, houses, clothes, land, businesses, or any of the other material things we value. Only what we have done for Christ will have validity. God will look at your fruit and based on God's judgment you will either spend an eternity in God's presence (heaven) or absent from God's glory (hell). It is our responsibility to bear fruit, to be a blessing, to lead soul's to Christ, to work as unto the Lord, to give to the kingdom on earth, to train up our children in the way they should go, to bear the infirmities of the weak, to mourn with those who mourn, to visit the afflicted, to take care of the widow and to worship and praise God. This is our fruit and this is our purpose!

But listen not only must we be fruitful we must also recognize that the Bible mandates us to multiply our fruit. You see, in every fruit there lies a seed. If that seed is nourished, it can be taken and planted somewhere else and another fruit tree can grow. The seed that we discover within our fruit is the knowledge of God. That's why it's so important to spread the Good News. It's not simply enough to do good and not give God the credit. So let me make this thing plain. I am a student who has many teachers including Mother, Father, Childhood pastor, and Seminary professors. In one way or another they have all taught me about the love and power of God. A seed was planted and because of them I've given my life completely to Christ. Now when I matured in Christ, I had the responsibility to plant that same seed in others. I plant it in the classroom with children. I plant it when I teach and preach at Women's Conference's, Retreats, and other services and with every life that I introduce to Christ or help to mature in the Lord. You see, the principle of multiplication is at work. And so I ask the question, "Are you multiplying the seed that was planted in you?"

STEPS TO PURSUING YOUR PURPOSE

Once you have determined that you will pursue your purpose, there are some simple steps you can take toward reaching this goal. One of the first ways to discover your purpose in the world is to simply ask God. Through *communication* or *prayer,* between you and God, you can discover your purpose. The reason many people can't hear their purpose through prayer is due to the fact that there are simply too many other voices competing for their attention. When you find that God seems silent before you, it could be that you are allowing God's voice to be drowned out by other voices. Listen, it is true that God speaks in a still, small voice and many times the radio, CD players, DVD players, television, cell phone, your co-workers, the kids, the traffic, etc., are drowning out the voice of God. Thus we see the need for fasting. Food fasts are simply one form of fasting. Fasting comes in many forms. There are times when we need to fast from the voices around us. In other words, make a covenant with yourself that you will not watch the media, listen to any music, or talk to anyone, other than when necessary, until you have heard from the Lord. When you do this, you will discover that you enjoy the atmosphere created by fasting and you are able to hear God's voice more clearly. I find that when I walk on nature trails and allow only the sounds of nature to permeate my being - God's voice is clearly audible to my soul. The Bible says we have not because we ask not. Perhaps many are still searching for their purpose and their peace because they haven't asked for it from God.

Secondly, you must look at what God has *created* in you. Your gifts and talents speak to your purpose. They were given to you so that when you are prepared to finally step into your purpose you will feel genuineness and ease with what God has placed you here to do. God doesn't gain pleasure from watching us struggle in this life. God has given us everything that we need to live out our purpose and destiny with dignity. That means we don't have to beg, borrow or steal anything to achieve God's design for our lives. Everything we need is already in us. It is our job to discover our gifts and talents and then cultivate that which we have discovered. It is for this reason that you should take a spiritual gifts inventory. I suggest that you take the Spiritual Gifts Inventory and Analysis on line at www.womenofdestiny.org. Once you have done this, you will be able to ascertain where your interests and gifts lie and thereby give your reasonable service to the Lord through your church.

Thirdly, you must *celebrate* not only your purpose in life but other's purpose as well. It is not simply enough for you to discover your purpose and gloat. You mustn't possess the attitude, "I've got mine, now you get yours." Believe it or not you didn't pull yourself up by your own bootstraps; there were others who provided you with the boots and the straps. The fact is you are your sister's keeper. Also when you honor your ancestors, you are celebrating the purpose of others. When you allow your gifts to be used for others, you are celebrating their purpose. Think about it, were you excited or disappointed the last time you discovered a friend had done well? You must celebrate other's purpose as you celebrate your own. Then and only then will your purpose be free to soar to unimaginable heights.

Fourth and finally you must *claim* your purpose. I know this sounds simple, however many people are unable to do this because their friends or family members can't see what God has placed in them. Many of you reading this book know what God is requiring of you. You are clear about your purpose, but you are afraid that people will think you are crazy if you leave that high paying job, or take on leadership in that ministry at church. You are afraid of being ridiculed, or perhaps you are afraid of failing. The only failure is in not trying - not stepping out - not pursuing your purpose. If I were you, I would be more afraid of living my entire life in a place not reserved for me. God has a **palace** of blessings reserved for you, but fear has caused you to settle for a **one room hotel**. I don't know about you, but I want all that God has reserved for me. Every day of laughter, joy, peace, prosperity and power, I want.

There truly is nothing more rewarding, exhilarating, and divine then living out your purpose for life. Today is your day to claim your purpose and thereby claim your blessings. Let me close this chapter by borrowing from a famous commercial and ask, "Got Purpose?" You are "Women of Destiny" which means that you must begin to discover your God-Purpose.

GROWTH THROUGH CONTEMPLATION
"WHY AM I HERE?"

1. Do you struggle with knowing your purpose in life?

2. What did your spiritual gifts inventory reveal to you about yourself that you didn't know?

3. Do you believe that God has something God wants you to do that no one else can do?

4. Are you willing to use your gifts in the church? Why or Why not?

5. List some of the fruit you have produced by your life (Ex., mentoring relationships, souls led to Christ, prisoners given hope, etc.).

6. Do you feel that you need to bear more fruit for God?

7. Are you intentional about keeping God at the center of all that you do so that your fruit is multiplied (i.e., do you share the gospel with everyone in all situations)?

8. Do you communicate with God to discover your purpose? If so, what has God revealed to you?

9. Do you believe that fasting could help you in discovering and understanding your purpose?

10. If you know your purpose in life, have you fully claimed and embraced it?

CHAPTER FIVE

God-
EMPOWERED

"But ye shall receive power, after that the Holy Ghost is
come upon you: and ye shall be witnesses unto me in Jerusalem, and in all Judea,
and in Samaria, and unto the uttermost parts of the earth."
ACTS 1: 8 (KJV))

I will never forget the day I met Tiffany. I was serving as a counselor in one of suburban Atlanta's largest Baptist churches. A young lady phoned me and through the quiet voice of one trying to hide from an assaulter, she asked if she could meet with me. We set a counseling appointment and little did I know that my life and the life of a young twenty-two year-old woman would change forever. When she showed up for the appointment she reminded me of someone who was in a witness protection program. Now that I reflect on it, perhaps she was a witness to the horrible devastation that the enemy can bring to one's life. She was dressed in dark oversized clothing. She wore a wig, no make-up and it looked as if her eye was bruised. She brought along her young daughter and she began to share her story with me. It was a story of abuse, assault and manipulation by her lover. She was looking for a way out, but more than that she was looking for the strength to get out. She tried to put the focus on her daughter's behavior at school and she shared with me that her daughter was having nightmares and that her grades were suffering. In the spirit of any counselor I began asking her questions about their home life. Soon I discovered that this beautiful, talented young lady was living in a homemade prison. Her boyfriend was physically and verbally abusive and she didn't know how to leave him. I was confronted with something I had never dealt with before. I assumed that all little girls were raised to think so highly of themselves that they would never let a man hit them. But to my surprise, this young lady was raised the same way but had found herself in a situation that she didn't know how to escape from. At each session we would talk about a plan of escape. I would do everything in my power to show her who she really was and how beautifully and wondrously she was made. I began to see her attitude change and before long she had escaped, unharmed, with her daughter. She became more involved in the life of the church and her daughter began to excel in school. Five years later, this same young lady went through the first Women of Destiny Faith Formation Program and on the final night she shared with the class that her desire today is to counsel abused women and help them to escape from the men that threaten their existence, and persecute their purpose. Her destiny is clear. God brought her out so that she might bring other women out. Now that's God-Empowered.

WHEN POWER MEETS PURPOSE

All of my adult life, I've desired to live a life that leaves a legacy. I call it becoming God-Empowered because it suggests a life of authority, influence, and power. When we speak of being God-Empowered, we are referring to women reaching a place in their lives when they are embodied with spiritual power and authority from God; such that they are able to reach their God *potential* and spiritually self-actualize. This means that they will achieve their ultimate destiny and be fulfilled, whole, prosperous, and leave a legacy in their homes, community and the world.

Potential can also be defined as "promise", which suggests that we can actually reach a place in our living where the *promises* of God are made manifest. I'm not certain about you, but I want to live a God-Empowered life so that my life affects people in such a way that my encounter with them forever changes them for the good. I want to live a life that causes the depressed to be delivered, that brings healing to the ailing, that brings sight to the spiritually blind, that engenders hope in the hopeless, that encourages the weary to run on to see what the end will be.

I vividly remember my childhood during the late sixties and early seventies. I remember the stories my father shared with my two older brothers and I when we would visit his hometown in the rural South. He would share with us the struggles he encountered growing up as an African American in the Deep South. These stories of my father's life empowered me and caused me to look at the world differently and reach beyond the ordinary to the extraordinary. I remember when other little girls my age where dreaming of being Ms. America, I wanted to be a guest on the Oprah Winfrey Show. Oprah started interviewing important people on a show in Baltimore called "People Are Talking." Then she moved to Chicago, started a local talk show, and grew in popularity to the degree that it became syndicated and bore her name, "The Oprah Winfrey Show." I always wanted to be a guest on that show, but not just any guest. I wanted to be a guest who would have something meaningful and life changing to offer. I wanted to be a person who gave so much of myself and my God-given talents, that my life would speak volumes on its own. My dream was that my life would become a legacy, an inheritance to future generations. I wanted to be God-Empowered and clearly be able to say, "I ran the race that was set before me, I stayed the course, and I ran it well!"

I don't know about you, but I want to be God-Empowered, not so that my ego can be stroked and my head egotistically enlarged. I want to be God-Empowered so that some child will be encouraged to climb the mountain of impossibility and move from the ghetto to the surgery room like Ben Carson. I want to be God-Empowered so that some woman will begin to see herself as the eagle she is, able to soar to the highest heights and bring others along with her like Harriet Tubman. I want my words to be written down so that one day people will read them and become so inspired that they recognize its power to change worlds like Maya Angelou. I want to be God-Empowered so that my life will cry out long after I'm gone, "A'int I a Woman!" like that of Sojourner Truth.

I'm certain that there is someone out there like me who never really desired to live the "popular life." That's the life where you seek to have everyone like you, and have more friends that you can keep up with. There is someone reading this work even now who doesn't want to live the "limelight life." This is the life that's lived 15-20-25 minutes in the spotlight but really has no meaning or substance (e.g., Monica Lewinsky, Anna Nicole Smith, or much of Hollywood for that matter). You see, this is the life that eventually fades into the backdrop as soon as someone flashier or more scandalous appears on the scene. We don't want to live the "party life" where every hour is happy hour and you end up as the person others laugh at because you're still trying to hang out with the young folk in your old age.

Instead, "Women of Destiny" should desire to live the "God-Empowered life." This is the life that is left as a gift for future generations to open, discover, be inspired and enlightened by, edify, and enjoy. This is the life that Jesus lived. This is the life that has such an impact on the world that your name is written in the annals of time and eternity. This is the life that looks beyond itself and gives to everyone around it. The life that shines in darkness, that smiles in sadness, that heals the hurting, that feeds the hungry, that lifts those left behind, that sees the invisible, and achieves the impossible. We must desire to live the God-Empowered life!

This book has provided you with the modus operandi for living that life. However, you must be responsible for applying what you have read to your life, to make your life count for something. African Americans are always saying, "All of our leaders are dead." This is not true. You are that leader. When you recognize that God has something special, extraordinary, unique, exceptional, rare and divine planned for your life you will begin to wrestle with the question, "Will I accept this challenge and become God-Empowered or will I vacillate, fluctuate, hesitate, procrastinate and end up living an empty existence?" You know about this empty existence don't you? It's life characterized by a monotonous routine of wake up, go to a dead end, unfulfilling job, drive home, eat dinner, watch a bad television show, go to bed, get up the next day and start all over again. This is not how God planned for you to live out your being. God desires that you become God-Empowered and that you possess the power to change the world around you.

The various life components (God-Produced, God-Positioned, God-Partnered, and God-Purposed) are areas that you must continually struggle to balance and achieve. In every new context whether a new job, new relationship, new church home, etc. you must struggle to achieve balance. Unfortunately, it is a never-ending struggle, sometimes filled with tears, pain, sadness, guilt, anger and remorse. Conversely, the struggle is filled with joy, triumph, beauty, gladness, and victory. The question is not, "Will I struggle?" The question is "How will I draw strength from the struggle?" "Women of Destiny" recognize that these areas of their lives must be navigated and negotiated by God. They come to understand that they are entirely too weak, uninformed, fickle, and fearful to achieve balance in these areas of their lives alone. And that is why prayer (two-way communication with God) is so important.

"Women of Destiny" are women who have figured out that they can do all things through *Christ* who gives them strength. They have reconciled that Christ came to this earth for the purpose of empowering them. You see, that's what Calvary was all about. With every pounding of the nails, Jesus was becoming God-Empowered. With every drop of blood that dripped from his thorn-crowned brow, he was receiving more authority and power. With every insult that was hurled at him, he was redeeming the lost. When they pierced him in his side, he was leading us home to the Lord. When they placed him in a borrowed tomb, he was setting us up for a blessing. When he got up early on Sunday morning, with all power in his hands, he had become God-Empowered and now through him we have everlasting life. But the greatest thing Christ did for us was to leave us this promise that "Greater works than this shall you do." So "Women of Destiny", never stop reaching until you become God-Empowered and see what great things the Lord has in store for you.

Langston Hughes, a great poet, wrote a poem entitled, "Negro Mother" that embodies a life that has become God-Empowered. It reads as follows:

> Children, I come back today
> To tell you a story of the long dark way
> That I had to climb, that I had to know
> In order that the race might live and grow.
>
> Look at my face - dark as the night -
> Yet shining like the sun with love's true light.
> I am the child they stole from the sand
> Three hundred years ago in Africa's land.
>
> I am the dark girl who crossed the wide sea
> Carrying in my body the seed of the free.
> I am the woman who worked in the field
> Bringing the cotton and the corn to yield.
>
> I am the one who labored as a slave,
> Beaten and mistreated for the work I gave-
> Children sold away from me, husband sold, too.
> No safety, no love, no respect was I due

Three hundred years in the deepest South:
But God put a song and a prayer in my mouth.
God put a dream like steel in my soul.
Now, through my children, I'm reaching the goal.

Now, through my children, young and free,
I realize the blessings denied to me.
I couldn't read then. I couldn't write.
I had nothing, back there in the night.

Sometimes, the valley was filled with tears,
But I kept trudging on through the lonely years.
Sometimes, the road was hot with sun,
But I had to keep on till my work was done:

I had to keep on! No stopping for me -
I was the seed of the coming Free.
I nourished the dream that nothing could smother
Deep in my breast - the Negro mother.

I had only hope then, but now through you,
Dark ones of today, my dreams must come true:
All you dark children in the world out there,
Remember my sweat, my pain, my despair.

Remember my years, heavy with sorrow -
And make of those years a torch for tomorrow!
Make of my past a road to the light
Out of the darkness, the ignorance, the night.

Lift high my banner out of the dust.
Stand like free men supporting my trust.
Believe in the right, let none push you back,
Remember the whip and the slaver's track.

Remember how the strong in struggle and strife
Still bar you the way, and deny you life -
But march ever forward, breaking down bars.
Look ever upward at the sun and the stars.

Oh, my dark children, may my dreams and my prayers
Impel you forever, up the great stairs -
For I will be with you till no white brother
Dares keep down the children of the Negro mother.

Women of Destiny know that you are God-Produced, God-Positioned, God-Partnered, God-Purposed and on your way to becoming God-Empowered. Your life has great meaning, and what God has for you to do, no one else can do. You are a "Woman of Destiny", no one can derail you. You are a "Woman of Destiny", you have the blood of queens running through your veins. You are a "Woman of Destiny", you know how to love, honor and respect those around you. You are a "Woman of Destiny" God is not through blessing you! You are a "Woman of Destiny" no weapon formed against you shall prosper. You are a woman of what? That's right, DESTINY! Eyes have not seen, ears have not heard, neither hath it entered into the heart of man what the Lord has in store for you!

10 WAYS TO KNOW IF YOU ARE GOD-EMPOWERED

You'll know that you are God-Empowered if:

1. You fear no man, no thing, only God. (2 Timothy 1:7, Psalm 27:1)

2. Your confidence is in God and not in yourself. (1 John 5:14)

3. You approach every day with joy and not sadness. (Nehemiah 8:10)

4. Your life has the power to change the world around you and leave a legacy. (I Corinthians 11: 24, Hebrews 6:10)

5. You receive the promises of God. (Hebrews 6: 12)

6. Faith guides your thoughts, actions, and beliefs and not foolishness. (2 Timothy 4: 7)

7. You recognize that you are never alone. (Hebrews 13:5)

8. You can draw strength from your struggle. (Psalm 28:7-9)

9. God is moving mightily in your life. (1John 4:4, Ephesians 3:20)

10. You are a servant. (John 12:26, Matthew 25: 21, Galatians 5:13, Acts 20:35)

GROWTH THROUGH CONTEMPLATION
"DO I POSSESS THE POWER?"

1. Do you understand what it means to be spiritually self-actualized?

2. What major life events have occurred that have kept you from being God-Empowered?

3. How do you believe your life will change when you become spiritually self-actualized?

4. Do you feel that you will be comfortable with your life when this happens?

5. What other women have inspired you to become God-Empowered? Why?

6. What characteristics do you feel you will possess when you become God-Empowered?

7. How will the lives of people around you change when you become God-Empowered?

8. If women during slave times were able to become God-Empowered what excuse can you give for not reaching yours?

JOURNALING

TOWARD WHOLENESS

DIRECTIONS: As you have been keeping a journal from the beginning of this book, today you will be asked to share with your classmates. In your journal you were to write your thoughts, feelings, questions and concerns as you ventured through each chapter. Your assignment is to share from your journal how this journey has impacted your life. Talk about any changes you have experienced in your self-concept and how you view yourself as a woman. Give voice to the insecurities that have kept you living in fear of living out your God-Purpose. What is shared is done so in the strictest of confidence as we commit to bring healing and wholeness to the body of believers.

GLOSSARY OF TERMS

Call - religious duty or vocation regarded as divinely inspired.

Faith - complete trust, confidence, or reliance; unquestioned belief in God.

Formation - The act of forming or making; the act of creating or causing to exist; the operation of bringing things together, or shaping or giving form.

God-Partnered - Our divine associations with others that help us to fulfill our God-Purpose.

God-Positioned - One's place or standing in the world as determined by God.

God-Produced - that which the Eternal has brought forward, given existence to, yielded, and created as an offering for others to view, notice and appreciate.

God-Purposed - That which is designed, resolved, and set before an individual to be reached or accomplished according to God's intent for their lives.

God-Empowered - When one reaches a place in their lives when they are embodied with power and authority from God; having spiritual power such that you are able to reach your God potential.

Modus Operandi - a method of procedure or operation.

Raison d'être - one's reason or justification for existence, literally interpreted from the French as "reason for being."

Religious Sexism - the behaviors, conditions, and attitudes in the church that foster stereotypes of social roles based on sex.

Self-esteem - belief in oneself; self-respect, self-love.

Self-knowledge - To have a clear and certain perception of oneself; to understand oneself based on the accumulation of information perceived or grasped by the mind.

Spiritual gifts - That which is given or bestowed upon you by God for the purpose of fulfilling a divine purpose; a spiritual quality or endowment conferred by God.

Spiritual Self-actualization - achieving one's ultimate destiny in life; recognizing one's power, authority and influence in the world.

Theology of Relationship - an understanding of God that emphasizes the importance and relevance of being with God and others.

PROGRAM SYLLABUS

YOUR CHURCH/ORGANIZATION'S NAME OR LOCATION

COURSE OBJECTIVE

The purpose of this program is to assist women in discovering their true identities and to help them make the most of their God-given talents and gifts. Given the reality that many women are not understanding and embracing their purpose/call in life due to historical, societal, and even religious constraints, and based on the Biblical premise that all should come into an understanding and acceptance of God's will for their lives, this program will educate and empower women, thus enabling them to respond and ultimately fulfill God's call on their lives.

MATERIALS NEEDED

1. *"Women of Destiny: Five Principles for Pursuing Your Purpose in God"* Lisa M. Tait, Author.
2. The Holy Bible, any version.
3. *"Woman of Destiny Journal,"* Lisa M. Tait, Author.

ASSIGNMENTS

-Weekly assigned readings.
-Class Participation
-"Growth Through Contemplation" Assignments
-Journaling: Should be done each week after class & readings.

ASSIGNMENT	ASSIGNED READING
CLASS I DATE	THEME: Introduction of the Program & Review Syllabus VISUAL LEARNING COMPONENT: "The Color Purple" ASSIGNED READING: Introduction, Prologue and Chapter One ASSIGNMENT: Answer questions from Visual Learning Exercise & Growth Through Contemplation - Chapter 1
CLASS II DATE	THEME: Chapter One - "God-Produced" VISUAL LEARNING COMPONENT ASSIGNED READING: Chapter Two ASSIGNMENT: Answer questions from Visual Learning Exercise & Growth Through Contemplation - Chapter 2
CLASS III DATE	THEME: Chapter Two - "God-Positioned" VISUAL LEARNING COMPONENT ASSIGNED READING: Chapter Three ASSIGNMENT: Answer questions from Visual Learning Exercise & Growth Through Contemplation - Chapter 3
CLASS IV DATE	THEME: Chapter Three - "God-Partnered" VISUAL LEARNING COMPONENT ASSIGNED READING: Chapter Four ASSIGNMENT: Answer questions from Visual Learning Exercise & Growth Through Contemplation - Chapter 4

CLASS V

DATE _____

THEME: Chapter Four - "God-Purposed"
VISUAL LEARNING COMPONENT
ASSIGNED READING: Chapter Five,
ASSIGNMENT: Answer questions from Visual
Learning Exercise & Growth Through
Contemplation - Chapter 5

CLASS VI

DATE _____

THEME: Chapter Five - "God-Empowered"
JOURNALING SHARING
ASSIGNMENT: Essay "Where Do We Go From
Here?" Participants share their experience of
this program

CLASS VII

DATE _____

THEME: "Where Do We Go From Here?" &
Participant Sharing
DISCUSSION TOPIC: "Where Do We Go From
Here?"

CLASS VIII

DATE _____

THEME: Closing Program
PROGRAM EVALUATION & RECEPTION

PROGRAM GUIDE

SESSION I
GOD-PRODUCED

Overall Objective: To help women define themselves and see that they are made in the image and likeness of God.

Goals:

1. To increase Biblical understanding of the creation of women.

2. To increase knowledge of what it means to be made in the image and likeness of God (Imageo Dei).

3. To begin to look outside of the restrictive boundaries that society has placed on its definition of women.

4. To begin to transfer this new understanding of creation as it directly relates to our own personal understanding of self.

5. To begin to examine some of our self-negating thoughts and behaviors due to a lack of this knowledge.

6. To become empowered by this knowledge of self in God.

Methods:

1. Present and discuss relevant Biblical details regarding the creation of women.

2. To gain a clear understanding on how society defines women.

3. Talk about the various ways in which to incorporate a new understanding of our being into our everyday lives.

4. Brainstorm and list the various ways in which a lack of this knowledge of self manifests itself in our thoughts and our behaviors.

Resources:

1. Biblical & extra-Biblical literature pertaining to women. Film and slides detailing the rich ancestral beginnings of African American women.

2. The DVD of "The Color Purple" by Alice Walker.

3. Program facilitator.

SESSION II
GOD-POSITIONED

Overall Objective: To help women discover their place in the world; "unmasking, disentangling and debunking" systems of oppression that place restrictions and boundaries on women.

Goals:

1. To increase participants knowledge of the importance of women in society and in the world.

2. To increase Biblical understanding of hierarchies and favoritism.

3. To begin to dialogue on the effects that embracing systems of oppression have on women.

4. To increase the participant's level of self-awareness and self-esteem such that they are able to employ the "Ten Principles of Black Self-Esteem" by E. Hammond Oglesby into their lives.

5. To clearly define the "isms" that society has created to keep certain persons (namely women) in subservient roles.

Methods:

1. Present and discuss relevant Biblical details regarding hierarchies and systems of oppression.

2. Discuss relevant scenes from "The Color Purple."

3. Have the participants research one woman who historically unmasked systems of oppression to leave a rich legacy for all women (e.g., Sojourner Truth, Harriet Tubman, Mary McCloud Bethune, Oprah Winfrey, Marian Anderson, Margaret Burroughs, Maya Angelou, Ruby Dee, Betty Shabazz, Fannie Lou Hamer, Alice Walker, Shirley Chisholm, etc,).

Resources:

1. Biblical and extra-Biblical literature.

2. The DVD of "The Color Purple" by Alice Walker.

3. Handout on the "Ten Principles of Black Self-Esteem."

4. Encyclopedia, texts or research material on a relevant African American woman in history.

5. Program facilitator.

SESSION III
GOD-PARTNERED

Overall Objective: To assist women in developing partnerships (i.e., friendships, mentoring relationships, models for parenting, intimate relationships) with others that will ultimately enhance their ability to live out their purpose.

Goals:

1. To educate women on the importance of developing partnerships with others who will help them to achieve their purpose in life.

2. To increase participant's understanding of the Biblical mandate to partner with one another.

3. To begin to look soberly at why tensions exist in female to female relationships.

4. To provide participant's with clear cut goals and character traits to look for when selecting friends.

Method:

1. Present and discuss relevant Biblical details and extra-Biblical literature dealing with the importance of relationships.

2. Group discussions on the relevance of interpersonal relationships.

3. To begin to examine some of the self-negating thoughts and behaviors due to a lack of quality relationships.

Resources:

1. Bible, any version, extra-Biblical literature.

2. DVD of the movie "The Color Purple" showing the relationship between the various women.

3. Group discussion including personal testimonies of the importance or lack thereof regarding relationships.

4. Program facilitator.

SESSION IV
GOD-PURPOSED

Overall Objective: To help women discover their purpose or reason for being (raison d'être).

Goals:

1. To enlighten the participants to the reality that all persons are gifted by God.

2. To increase participants understanding of their spiritual gifts and talents.

3. To understand the various ways in which our spiritual gifts can be used daily to build the Kingdom of God.

4. The women should be able to answer the question, "Why am I here?" and "What was I created to do?"

Methods:

1. Through the use of Biblical passages and extra-Biblical literature we will examine God's intent for humankind.

2. Through the results of the On-line Spiritual Gifts Inventory participants will gain greater insight as to their spiritual gifts and talents.

3. Review and discuss points learned about the nine spiritual gifts (evangelism, prophecy, teaching, exhortation, Pastor/Shepherd, showing mercy, serving, giving, and administration).

4. Discuss how these spiritual gifts can be used in the church and community.

Resources:

1. Spiritual Gifts Inventory and Analysis at www.womanofdestiny.org

2. The DVD of "The Color Purple" by Alice Walker.

3. Bible, any version and extra-Biblical literature.

4. Program facilitator.

SESSION V
GOD-EMPOWERED

Overall Objective: To help women reach a place in their lives where they are embodied with power and authority from God; having spiritual power such that they are able to reach their God potential and spiritually self-actualize.

Goals:

1. To show women that spiritual self-actualization is our primary goal in life.

2. To have participants begin to examine where they are on this journey toward being God-Empowered.

3. To allow the women to explore their rich heritage and understand their legacy of being God-Empowered through the poetry of Langston Hughes.

4. To look at those issues and life altering events that hinder our progress in becoming God-Empowered.

Method:

1. Present and discuss relevant Biblical details and extra-Biblical literature regarding spiritual self-actualization.

2. To gain a clear understanding of the process of becoming God-Empowered.

3. Brainstorm and discuss the various ways in which our issues have delayed us from being God-Empowered.

4. Through discussion of each participant's journaling we will examine where the ladies are in their quest of being God-Empowered.

Resources:

1. Bible, any version.

2. PowerPoint presentation of Biblical examples of women who were God-Empowered.

3. Program facilitator.

VISUAL LEARNING GUIDE

CHAPTER ONE
VISUAL LEARNING EXERCISE

Directions: Watch the following scenes of "The Color Purple" in class 2 & 3 (Side A) (Winter 1909: Celie gives birth, and Celies's prayers) on DVD. **Do not watch** any other scenes of the movie. Begin to ask yourself the following questions based on the movies content:

1. What impact did having an abusive father have on Celie and her understanding of self?
2. What labels had society and family placed on Celie?
3. What specific life events could have hindered her from discovering her authentic being?
4. What do you believe kept her in search of the knowledge of her true self as opposed to just giving up?
5. What role did God play in Celie's quest for self-knowledge?

CHAPTER TWO
VISUAL LEARNING EXERCISE

Directions: Watch the following scenes of "The Color Purple" in class (Side A) 5 - 9, 11-12 (Celie's new home, Spring 1909: Celie sees her baby, Nettie comes to stay, Spelling lesson, Albert makes his move; sisters parted, Harpo & Sofia, and Domestic disputes) on DVD. **Do not watch** any other scenes of the movie. Begin to ask yourself the following questions based on the movies content:

1. How did Celie understand her position in the home? Did she feel powerful or powerless?

2. What roles and responsibilities had been relegated to Celie as the woman of the house?

3. Have these roles changed much since 1909?

4. How was Nettie different from Celie in her understanding of her role in life? What caused these differences?

5. What do you believe were Celie's greatest obstacles in achieving her rightful place in the world?

6. What issues did Celie develop because of her perceived position in the world?

CHAPTER THREE
VISUAL LEARNING EXERCISE

Directions: Watch the following scenes of "The Color Purple" in class (Side A) 13, 19, and 21 ("You told Harpo to beat me!" Miss Celie's Blues, and Shug and Celie: "He beat me for not being you") on DVD. **Do not watch** any other scenes of the movie. Begin to ask yourself the following questions based on the movies content:

1. What were the dynamics of the relationship between Celie and Sofia, between Celie and Shug?

2. Do we find that friends often transfer the dysfunction from their relationship onto your relationships (i.e., they are abused and therefore you should also be abused)?

3. What was Celie lacking in her current relationships that she found in her relationship with Shug?

4. Did you gain a sense that Alice Walker was trying to emphasize the importance of women having supportive friendships?

CHAPTER FOUR
VISUAL LEARNING EXERCISE

Directions: Watch the following scenes of "The Color Purple" in class (Side B) 11, 13- 15 (Dinner: Celie's curse on Albert, Funeral; Celie comes home, Maybe God Is Tryin' to tell You Something, Albert's redemption, The family reunited). **ADVISORY:** There is profanity used in one scene. **Do not watch** any other scenes of the movie. Begin to ask yourself the following questions based on the movies content:

1. What do you believe occurred in the movie that caused Celie to seek after her purpose?

2. How did her family and friends play a role in the discovery of her purpose?

3. What did Celie mean in her statement, "I'm Black, I'm a woman, and I may even be ugly, but I'm here, I'm here"!

4. How did Celie's life change when she began her quest for her God-Purpose?

5. What role did the church play in Shug ultimately recognizing her God-Purpose?

6. How would Celie's life had differed if she had stayed with Mister?

EVALUATION FORM

NAME (OPTIONAL)

DATE

Directions: Please answer the questions on a scale from 1 - 5.
1=Not at all, 3=Somewhat, 5=Yes or exceeded expectations.

QUESTIONS	CIRCLE YOUR RESPONSE
1. Do you feel like this course helped to develop or strengthen your faith?	1 2 3 4 5
2. Do you feel that the information presented helped you to discover your true identity?	1 2 3 4 5
3. Did this Program help you to make the most of your God-given talents and gifts?	1 2 3 4 5
4. Was the material presented in a manner that you could easily understand?	1 2 3 4 5
5. Did the facilitator seem to have knowledge of the material presented?	1 2 3 4 5
6. Did you like the way the class was structured (journals, group discussions, teaching and video)?	1 2 3 4 5

7. Was the book helpful to you?   1   2   3   4   5

8. Would you recommend this book   1   2   3   4   5
or program to a friend?

9. Did this program challenge you to   1   2   3   4   5
change any aspect of your life?

10. Do you feel you have arrived at or
are on your way to recognizing your   1   2   3   4   5
power, authority and influence in the
world?

You may give your final thoughts in this section.

_____

_____

_____

_____

_____

_____

_____

_____

_____

_____

_____

_____

_____

_____

_____

_____

1. Since this program began have you become involved in a ministry in the church?

❑ Yes   ❑ No   If yes, what ministry _____

2. If you were already involved in a ministry in the church, did this program cause you to be more fully committed to it?

❑ Yes   ❑ No   ❑ Somewhat

3. If you are not already involved in a ministry in the church, do you plan on becoming involved in the near future?

❑ Yes   ❑ No

4. What suggestions would you make to improve this Faith Formation Program

❑ Longer class time

❑ Add more weeks to program

❑ Less teaching

❑ More teaching

❑ Less group discussion

❑ More group discussion

❑ More journal sharing

❑ More discussion of the "Color Purple"

❑ Other _____

BIBLIOGRAPHY

Akbar, Na'im. *Breaking the Chains of Psychological Slavery*. Tallahassee: Mind Productions & Associates, 1996.

Alexander, Amy. *Fifty Black Women Who Changed America*. Secaucas: Birch Lane Press, 1999.

Benjamin, T. Garrot. *Boys to Men: A Handbook for Survival*. Indianapolis: Heaven on Earth Publishing House, 1993.

Birchett, Colleen. *How to Help Hurting People*. Chicago: Urban Ministries, 1990.

Boyd, Julia. *In The Company of My Sisters: Black Women and Self-Esteem*. New York: Penguin Books, 1993.

Brown, Teresa L. Fry. *God Don't Like Ugly: African American Women Handing on Spiritual Values*. Nashville: Abingdon Press, 2000.

Cannon, Katie G. *Katies's Canon: Womanism and the Soul of the Black Community*. New York: Continuum Publishing Company, 2002.

_____. *Black Womanist Ethics*. Atlanta: Scholars Press, 1985.

Cook, Suzan Johnson. *Too Blessed To Be Stressed*. Nashville: Thomas Nelson Publishers, 1998.

Douglas, Kelly Brown. *Sexuality and the Black Church*. New York: Orbis Books, 1999.

Felder, Cain. *Troubling Biblical Waters: Race Class and Family.* New York: Orbis Books, 1989.

George, Elizabeth. *A Woman After God's Own Heart.* Eugene: Harvest House   Publishers, 1997.

Green, Jackie. *When She Hears The Call.* Phoenix: The Kuumba House, 1997.

Hare, Nathan & Julia. *Bringing the Black Boy to Manhood: The Passage.* San Francisco: Black Think Tank, 1985.

Hollies, Linda. *Jesus and Those Bodacious Women: Life Lessons from One Sister to Another.* Cleveland: Pilgrim Press, 1998.

_____. *Inner Healing For Broken Vessels: Seven Steps to a Woman's Way of Healing.* Nashville: Upper Room Books, 1992.

Hooks, Bell. *Talking Back: Thinking Feminist - Thinking Black.* Boston: South End Press, 1989.

_____. *Salvation: Black People and Love.* New York: Harper Collins Publishers, Inc., 2001.

_____. *Sisters of the Yam: Black Women and Self-Recovery.* Boston: South End Press, 1993.

Kimbrough, Marjorie. *She is Worthy: Encounters with Biblical Women.* Nashville: Abingdon Press, 1994.

Lewis, Mary C. *Herstory: Black Female Rites of Passage.* Chicago: African American Images, 1988.

Lightner, Ann Farrar. *And Your Daughters Shall Preach: Developing a Female Mentoring Program in the African American Church*. St. Louis: Hodale Press, Inc., 1995.

Matthews, Alice. *A Woman God Can Use*. Grand Rapids: Discovery House 1990.

McKenzie, Vashti. *Not Without a Struggle: Leadership Development for African American Women in Ministry*. Cleveland: United Church Press, 1996.

_____. *Journey to the Well*. New York: Viking Press, 2002.

McKnight, Reginald. *Wisdom of the African World*. Novato: The Classic Wisdom Collection, 1996.

Myers, William. *God's Yes Was Louder Than My No*. Trenton: Africa World Press, 1994.

Oglesby, E. Hammond. *Ten Principles of Black Self-Esteem: Letters of Heritage, Lessons of Hope*. Cleveland: The Pilgrim Press, 1999.

Painter, Nell I. *Sojourner Truth: A Life, a Symbol*. New York: W.W. Norton & Company, 1996.

Proctor, Samuel D. *Samuel Proctor: My Moral Odyssey*. Valley Forge: Judson, 1989.

Riggs, Marcia. *Awake, Arise & Act: A Womanist Call For Black Liberation*. Minneapolis: Fortress Press, 1994.

Townsend Gilkes, Cheryl. *If It Wasn't For The Women: Black Women's Experience and Womanist Culture in Church and Community*. Maryknoll: Orbis Books, 2001.

Weems, Renita J. *Battered Love: Marriage, Sex & Violence in the Hebrew Prophets.* Minneapolis: Fortress Press, 1995

_____. *I Asked For Intimacy: Stories of Blessings, Betrayals and Birthings.* San Diego: Luramedia, 1993.

_____. *Showing Mary: How Women Can Share Prayers, Wisdom, and the Blessings of God.* West Bloomfield: Warner Books, 2002.

Wimberly, Anne & Parker, E. *In Search of Wisdom: Faith Formation in the Black Church.* Nashville: Abingdon Press, 2002.

ARTWORK ORDERING INFO

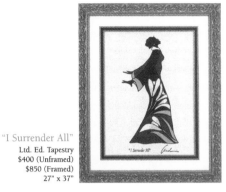

"I Surrender All"
Ltd. Ed. Tapestry
$400 (Unframed)
$850 (Framed)
27" x 37"

"Order My Steps"
Ltd. Ed. Tapestry
$400 (Unframed)
$850 (Framed)
27" x 37"

"What God Put Together"
Ltd. Ed. Tapestry
$350 (Unframed)
$750 (Framed)
17" x 25"

"If God Said It"
Ltd. Ed. Tapestry
$350 (Unframed)
$750 (Framed)
18" x 24"

"He's An Ontime God"
Ltd. Ed. Tapestry
$350 (Unframed)
$750 (Framed)
27" x 37"

ARTWORK BY ANDRE THOMPSON
To order visit: www.artbyandre.com
For Phone Orders Call: 404-396-4404

BOOK ORDERING INFO

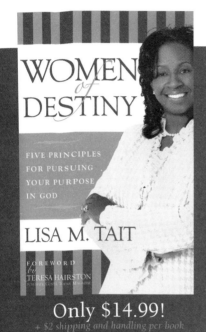

WOMEN *of* DESTINY

FIVE PRINCIPLES
FOR PURSUING
YOUR PURPOSE
IN GOD

LISA M. TAIT

FOREWORD *by*
TERESA HAIRSTON

Only $14.99!
+ $2 shipping and handling per book

COMPLETE ORDER FORM
AND MAIL TO:
5238 Ashley Drive, SW
Lilburn, GA 30047
USA

Money Orders and Checks should be made payable to: Women of Destiny Ministries

Credit Cards Accepted: Visa, MasterCard, American Express, Discover

Order On-line:
www.womenofdestiny.org

(Allow 2-3 weeks for delivery)

ORDER FORM

FIRST NAME   LAST NAME

ADDRESS

ADDRESS 2

CITY   STATE   ZIP CODE

PHONE NUMBER   EMAIL ADDRESS

CREDIT CARD TYPE: ❏ VISA   ❏ MASTERCARD   ❏ AMERICAN EXPRESS   ❏ DISCOVER

CREDIT CARD #   EXP. DATE

SIGNATURE   CREDIT CARD VERIF. # (3 DIGIT # ON BACK OF CARD)